Beyond Air Guitar

Beyond Air Guitar

A Rough Guide for Christian Students and Graduates in Art, Design and the Media

Alastair Gordon

with Susan Beresford, Norman Stone, Robert Orchardson, James Cary, Kieran Dodds, Interface Arts Relay Group, Rael Mason, Henningham Family Press, Rachel Nunson and Sparks

PiQUANT editions

First published in Great Britain by Piquant Editions in 2012

PO Box 83, Carlisle, CA3 9GR, UK

www.piquanteditions.com

ISBN 978-1903689-54-7

British Library Cataloguing in Publication Data

Gordon, Alastair.

Beyond air guitar : a rough guide for Christian students and graduates in art, design and the media.

1. Christianity and art. 2. Christian art and symbolism.

3. Christianity in mass media. 4. Artists--Religious life.

I. Title II. Beresford, Susan.

700.8'827-dc23

ISBN-13: 9781903689547

Cover design by Alastair Gordon

Book design by Dave Latcham

Typesetting by 2at.com

Dedicated to the Interface students and graduates

S.D.G.

Contents

LIFE AFTER ART COLLEGE

RESOURCES

A Few Words About This Book ...

If you are a Christian and an artist this book is for you. It has been designed
as a working handbook with a particular leaning towards the visual arts and
design. I have written specifically with students and graduates in mind but I
hope that the book will also be of use to more mature artists, as a refresher of
foundational ideas or perhaps to spark new inspiration for work and creative
practice. You can read it on your own or with a group. If you're in an art college
Christian Union, graduate fellowship or church art group you could use it as a
term programme. I hope this little guide will be of practical use in the studio
or to be read a chapter a day on the way to work. You can read it in the order
you find it or you can head straight to the bits that look most juicy. Either way I
hope it encourages you as much as it has me in going back to God's word to see
again his desires for art.

And a few thank yous ...

This book is a collaboration of ideas. I am indebted to other writers, greater than
I, such as Jeremy Begbie, Hilary Brand, Michael Card, Adrienne Chaplin, Terry
Eagleton, James Elkins, Suzi Gablik, E. H. Gombrich, Leen La Rivière, C. S.
Lewis, Hans Rookmaaker, Francis Schaeffer, Calvin Seerveld, Betty Spackman,
John Stott, David Thistlethwaite and Steve Turner.

The idea for this project came about through various discussions and events I
have been privileged to be involved with in UCCF: Interface Arts. If you've been
at one of these arts events in recent years the chances are that some of your
thoughts have been stolen, borrowed or begged for these pages. In particular, I
would like to thank Ellis Potter, Jim Paul, Edith Reitsema, Gavin McGrath, Peter
Smith, Luci Metcalfe and Cully. Thanks are also due to the Interface Arts Relay
crews over the years: Maz, Drew, Fraser, Issi, Ibi, Sara, Ed, James, Dan, Lois,
Lizzie, Holly, Rael, Millie, Matthew, Rupert and Ashleigh, who have stimulated
many great ideas. I hope I represent you well.

Some of the illustrations are my own, but several other artists have also
contributed work. I thank you all for your generous help: Lizzie Kevan
did subsequent work on most of the illustrations in part 1. Katie Akhurst

contributed the illustrations on page 75; Owain Shaw created the photographs for the chapter on Making Culture; Zoe Baker designed the illustrations for part 4; and finally, David Latcham designed the general book layout.

To those who have read, re-read and re-read again early drafts, I am extremely grateful for your patience in helping me iron out some of the more tricky parts. Thanks especially to Phil Allcock, Ruth Gordon, John Graham, Michael Laird, Gavin McGrath and Edward Mayhew, who have all helped in this way. Pieter and Elria Kwant deserve a particular thanks. Thank you for your help and patience through the process and for believing in this project.

My greatest thanks are to my wife, Anna, for your love, support and encouragement

Many thanks to you all.

Alastair Gordon
London

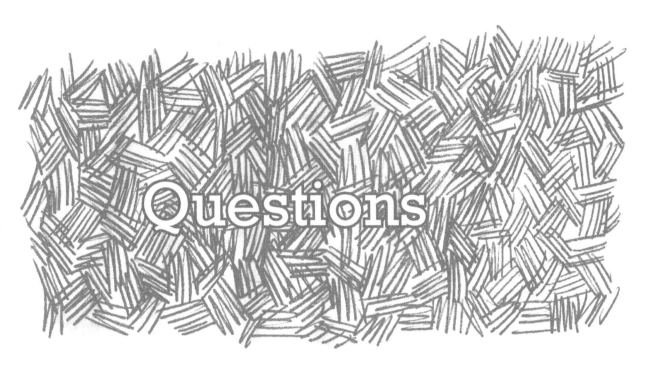

Questions

Every artist asks questions …

It's just what we do.

When we were children we asked questions all the time until our parents went blue in the face. Why, what, when, how, who—questions, questions, questions.

Jesus said we are to change and become like little children again (Matt 18:3). In a similar way the apostle Paul instructed the church in Thessalonica to 'Test everything' (1 Thess 5:21).

Asking questions is part of the way we understand the world, our God and who we are. Jesus himself asked lots of questions and it made some people feel nervous.

The ability to ask questions is a privilege shared by all human beings, and God encourages us to ask, probe and enquire. He even allowed Jacob to wrestle him in the middle of the night, and Jacob refused to let go until he received a blessing. We have questions for God but more important are the questions God has for us about how we live in his creation, how we relate to him and to one another and, for us artists, how we create.

In this book we will be asking a lot of questions about the creative arts and media, ourselves and the role of Christians in creative culture today. We will ask how Christians are and should be distinctive from other artists, how we are the same, what expectations we should have when we try to live for Christ in the arts, what should be normal for us and where the church can be radical in bringing Christ's message of redemption to the creative arts and media.

My hope in this book is to ask the kinds of questions we don't normally get the chance to ask as artists who are Christian. I fear I have more questions than answers but I believe that, sometimes, finding the right question can be more helpful than hurrying to find an answer. When there is a question an idea is still alive, but when there is an answer, especially the wrong answer, an idea is stopped dead.

Please test what you read in this book. Please ask questions with me. Perhaps together we can affirm how we should live as artists and what approaches to art-making give greatest glory to God.

Where else, then, would we start than by asking a question?

1. What is Christian Art?

(Sketch, doodle, draw. Make this title page your own.)

How to make your own kitsch art.

*Your guide to maintaining the status quo
and perpetuating stereotypes.*

1.

*You will need:
Coloured felt-tip pens or crayons.
Photographs of beautiful scenery, or scenes
 that look 'Biblical' such as deserts or donkeys.
Images of Jesus, his disciples or kittens.
A selection of well-known Bible verses.
A Laminator.*

To make your creation shiny, durable and wipe-clean, simply laminate it.

2.

*Depending on where you have obtained your
imagery (a magazine, the internet, your own
imagination) you can photocopy, scan or draw
your image onto a thin sheet of A4 paper
(optional pastel coloured). If you are using a
computer program, don't forget the wealth of
fonts at your fingertips.*

3.

*Whatever your imagery the Bible verse is the
key element. Place it in any of the four corners
- most traditionally the bottom right. Avoid the
centre as this will invaribly obscure the image.*

4.

*You may wish to display your creation for all
to see. Recommended locations include office
notice boards, church vestries (or kitchens), and
water closets. Avoid displays in the vicinity of
the culturally sensitive.*

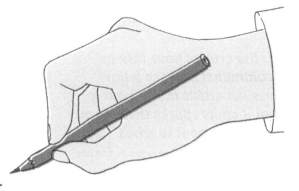

John 3:16

It is the crux of your task as a communal body of fellow christian artists to fire your art until it emits sparks that warm, or burn, those it reaches.

Calvin Seerveld, theologian and writer [1]

Beyond Air Guitar

Q: What words, pictures and ideas come to mind when you think of 'christian art'?

Why not put your own ideas down in the area below:

When you hear the term 'Christian art', your first thought might be towards fuzzy-felt banners or cheesy paintings of Jesus, or rainbows or kittens with inspiring Bible verses embossed underneath. Perhaps you think of stained glass windows or great works of art, visual, musical or written, made over the years by Christians such as Mendelssohn, Bach, Rembrandt, Cranach the Elder, Flora Macdonald or C. S. Lewis, to name just a few.

In the past the church has commissioned magnificent works of art that continue to be celebrated as part of our cultural heritage, but in contrast there are few artists working professionally in the creative arts and media today who openly profess belief in Christ. In a similar sense, though with the odd exception, we rarely hear of art being commissioned by local churches (and particularly from the evangelical tradition). We can't help but ask, 'Why?'

1.   *From chapter 2*, Bearing Fresh Olive Leaves *(Carlisle: Piquant, 2000), p. 35.*

Jesus on the cross (after Rembrandt)

Art historian James Elkins writes, 'Contemporary art, I think, is as far from organised religion as Western Art has ever been, and that may even be its most singular achievement—or its cardinal failure, depending on your point of view.'[2] My own experience tells me that the picture may not be as desperate as Elkins paints it but I think he is right to observe an unhealthy entrenchment between the art world and the church. Often the stereotype of art made by Christians involves notions of kitsch or sentimentality, or work that refers solely to church doctrines or dogma, not responsively to the issues and needs of contemporary culture. Elkins concludes, 'aside from the rare exceptions, religion is seldom mentioned in the art world unless it is linked to criticism, ironic distance, or scandal. An observer of the art world might well come to the conclusion that religious practice and religious ideas are not relevant to art unless they are treated with scepticism.'[3] The problem doesn't seem to be the inclusion of religious ideas, even symbols, in contemporary art but the sincere conviction that these ideas actually matter: that they mean something important, let alone describe something of truth, beauty and reality.

Landscapes, lamp-stands and lighthouses

Light in the darkness (after Thomas Kincade)

One famous Christian artist is Californian landscape painter Thomas Kinkade, who is arguably the most financially successful artist of his generation and who openly professes belief in Christ. Kinkade is the self-proclaimed 'painter of light' and his landscape paintings are reproduced and sold around the world through a vast network of franchise galleries and brand retail outlets. You've probably seen a few.

Kinkade paints romanticized landscapes, often depicting blooming gardens, inviting church buildings illuminated by elaborate lamp-

2. *From James Elkins,* On the Strange Place of Religion in Contemporary Art *(New York: Routledge, 2004), p. 15.*

3. *Elkins,* On the Strange Place of Religion in Contemporary Art, *p. 16.*

stands, or mountains and sunsets bathed in exaggerated pink glows from the setting sun; boats find shelter from stormy water and lighthouses guide the way for the lost. Kinkade paints an icthus and appropriate Bible verse in the bottom right-hand corner of each painting.

Whilst Kinkade's brand sells well across the world he doesn't enjoy a positive level of appreciation from the contemporary art world. Art critic Linda Weintraub writes,

> If he is exceptional, it is because he presents the values that many people share. He is a romantic idealist who prefers the homey to sublime, the past to the present, the rural to the urban, the sensual to the intellectual, the cheerful to the sorrowful ... His audience requires no convincing because he offers them the opportunity to remain complacent as they escape into a perfect dream world. In the presence of his paintings they revel in the status quo of their desires.[4]

Kinkade's work is widely dismissed by contemporary artists as kitsch or twee, and considered by many to be sentimental and tasteless. In her book *A Profound Weakness: Christians*

and Kitsch, artist Betty Spackman comments how this particular brand of Christian kitsch 'tends to reinforce ideas and convictions rather than either generate or challenge them and in this way has the function of reassuring the consumer or user and confirming their beliefs'.[5] The sheer demand for his work makes it obvious that Kinkade is supplying something that is certainly wanted, but, we might ask, is it really needed? Christian theologian Calvin Seerveld warns, 'Art, like anything else, is relevant if it supplies what is needed. Art that is popular is supplying what is wanted, but not necessarily what is needed, and may not, therefore, be relevant.'[6]

Preachers and promised lands

Kinkade works within a legacy of Christian art that is as complex in its history as it is diverse. Take, for example, the work of German Renaissance painter Cranach the Elder, who was good mates with the Protestant reformer Martin Luther. Luther commissioned Cranach to make art for his church in Wittenberg and Cranach's altar-piece was a spectacular visual demonstration of reformed theology. It represented Luther and his mates as apostles

4. *From Linda Weintraub,* Making Contemporary Art: How Today's Artists Think and Work *(London: Thames and Hudson, 2003), p. 21.*

5. A Profound Weakness: Christians and Kitsch *(Carlisle, UK: Piquant Editions, 2005), p. 5.*

6. *From chapter 2,* Bearing Fresh Olive Leaves, *p. 36.*

at the Last Supper receiving the bread and the wine from a Christian brother. Not only so, but it also illustrated the congregation hearing sermons in their own language, as opposed to the previous tradition of Latin. At the centre of the base panel is an image of Jesus on the cross, as if to say it is Christ who is being preached. This is a no-holds-barred illustration of Protestant Christian teaching. But the question remains, is it 'Christian art'?

Other artists have woven a Christian message into their art through the more subtle tools of allegory and suggestion. We might think of nineteenth-century Romantic painter Caspar David Friedrich and his sublime metaphorical landscapes of a world beyond our own, or C. S. Lewis's famous use of allegory in the Narnia novels. Others have taken a Christian theme such as redemption, hope or peace as a starting point for a work of art. But is it 'Christian art'?

Red pill, blue pill and street peddlers

I and my fellow art students in Glasgow became used to people stopping us in the street to ask us to sign up to one charity or another.

I was once stopped by a very enthusiastic man with a clipboard and optimistically coloured jacket wanting to talk to me about the film *The Matrix* that had just come out. To him, the film dealt with deeply religious ideas that even alluded to the meaning of life. I was just on my way for a quick bite to eat before my afternoon lecture and didn't really think I had the time to get into a street discussion on theology but I suspected from his patter that he might have had a discouraging morning, so I stopped to chat.

'I think life is like that film *The Matrix*,' he said, reaching for a pamphlet in his jacket pocket. 'You either take the way of the blue pill or the path of the red pill.'

I nodded my head in casual agreement and waited for him to tell me which church he was representing, but his next line came as a bit of a surprise.

'I am a Hindu and I believe the blue pill is the path towards eternity.' I couldn't believe it! Christians, it seems, are not the only ones who find hidden messages in films to match their own agendas.

If a film, song or painting deals with issues that allude to a spiritual realm, does that qualify it to be described as 'religious' or even 'Christian' art?

What do you think? Here are a few questions that might help open the discussion:

Q: List a few works of art that *you* think bring glory to God. What is it about them that you think glorifies God?

Q: Why do you think so many Christians are attracted to making and consuming kitsch art? What is 'kitsch' art anyway, and what do you think God makes of it?

Q: What other approaches to art-making have you seen among Christians? What do you think works? What doesn't?

No such thing as Christian art ...

In some ways the question of 'Christian art' is a bit of a false starter. Just as there is no such thing as 'Christian medicine', 'Christian food' or 'Christian plumbing', there is really no such thing as 'Christian art'. There may be Christians who are doctors, chefs, plumbers and artists but there really are no genres, styles, media or creative disciplines that can be defined exclusively as belonging to the Christian faith. For 'The earth is the Lord's and *everything* in it,' writes David (Ps 24:1; emphasis added) and 'everything God created is good, and nothing is to be rejected if it is received with thanksgiving, because it is consecrated by the word of God and prayer' (1 Tim 4:4,5).

Since all humans are made in the image of God all artists are capable of making great work, whether they are Christian or not. Just as those who don't know Christ personally have made art that will not bring him glory, so Christians have been responsible for some pretty terrible art too. A Christian can make art that is idolatrous just as a non-believer can make art that pleases God (and we will expand on these points as we go on).

...There are, however, Christian approaches to making art

The apostle Paul wrote, 'Whatever you do, work at it with all your heart, as working for the Lord, not for men' (Col 3:23). The Christian approach to art begins with working hard for the glory of God in whatever arena of the arts he leads us to be active within. As with every act of service to Christ, art-making requires some prayer, study and the renewing of our minds through the power of God's Spirit and his word. Artistic worship of Christ pushes us towards excellence both in the integrity and humility of our characters and in the hard graft of our work.

When God created the world it was 'very good'. The excellence and diversity of his creation can be seen all around us. It's an old adage but true nonetheless that when man freezes water he makes something dull and unimaginative like an ice cube, but when God freezes water he turns it into the most beautiful and intricate of shapes, each snowflake being unique and wonderfully made. Why would God do that unless he was interested in the aesthetic dimension of his creation? When Jesus turned water into wine at the wedding at Cana the guests

thought it was the finest wine they had ever tasted. He had the option of churning out any old brew (most guests, after all, were drunk and probably wouldn't have cared), but Jesus chose to give them the best.

Since we are made in the image of God and strive to live as Jesus did, surely our own creative offerings should be the very best we can offer. Perfection is not required but we are tasked, as Paul instructs, 'to work ... with all [our] heart, as ... for the Lord' (Col 3:23).

What art should we make?

The Christian is free to make art in any discipline, medium or genre he or she chooses. The diversity of subject matter available to the Christian is rainbow rich as illustrated by the magnificent variety of creative writing styles in the Bible itself, from the creation accounts of Genesis to John's apocalyptic Revelation.

If there's a misconception that Christians should be limited to making art that is 'safe' or 'nice' we need only look to the book of Judges, which demonstrates some pretty gruesome tales. Think of Jael and her tent peg, or poor King Eglon who came to his bloody end by the length of Ehud's sword, drawn deep within his belly by the traction of his own fat!

The line of Christian engagement in the arts is not drawn by particular subject matter, medium or style but through the rich instruction of God's word in the Bible, being constrained only by the limits of our imaginations and the sinful desires of vanity and ego. We are free to make art on any subject because God is active in every area of his creation. We are also free, however, not to make art on subjects that may be harmful to us or lead us to sin. We should pray for God's help in choosing what art to make and perhaps call on the advice of trusted friends in the hope that we might mature.

There is no story that is outside the authority of Jesus, no question or idea that is beyond his interest because 'all things were created by him and for him' (Col 1:16). There may be no such thing as 'Christian art' by definition but God is deeply interested in the way we live as artists and what we make for him because he is deeply concerned for every area of his creation and especially those who are made in his image. Over these following chapters let's dig deeper into his word and discover together what God's purposes are for art-making.

Q: What challenges and opportunities do you face as a Christian hoping to serve Christ in the arts? How can you pray for God's help?

Q: What limits your freedom as an artist who is a Christian?

2. What is Art Anyway?

(Sketch, doodle, draw. Make this title page your own.)

One of the phrases people frequently raise is: does it matter whether something is art? Who cares? Perhaps nothing is art, perhaps everything is. So what?

Flint Schier,
contemporary literary and art critic[7]

Q: How would you define art? Does art need a definition?

7. *From* Deeper
    Into Pictures
    *(Cambridge: CUP,
    1986), n.p.*

Definitions: paintings and poodles

Ask ten artists what they think art is and you're likely to get ten different answers. Some might say it's to do with human expression or something about skill and ability. Others might talk about art in terms of communication or language. Some might categorize art in terms of 'high' art (Art with a capital 'A') and 'low' or 'popular' art (art with a lower-case 'a'). A 'work of art' can be a painting, sculpture, building or musical score but it can also be a well-prepared meal, a pampered poodle or even a nasty person who is 'a real work of art'. Surely these things can't all be 'art'? Or can they?

Some might ask why we need to define art in the first place but for the purposes of our discussion it's important we at least have a sense of what we're talking about! Let's not get confused between paintings and poodles.

I sometimes struggle with definitions, finding them restrictive and, at times, limiting to the imagination, but a good definition can also open new possibilities. We could think of definitions as ideas existing alongside one another within a circle. There would definitely be an outside to the circle, for some definitions are clearly not correct, but there is also an inside, room for various possibilities to interact with one another inside the circle. Let's consider a few possibilities for what might be inside the circle of 'art' and what should stay outside.

1. An abbreviation (/abv.)

'Art' may be an abbreviation for the terms *creative arts* or *contemporary arts* and therefore incorporate the practices of visual art (such as painting, sculpture and graphic design), performance art (inclusive of music, dance and theatre), literary art (such as poetry and novels) and the media (including journalism, broadcasting and Internet art). This is a starting point.

2. To be literal (lit·er·al, adj)

The word 'art' comes from the Latin term *ars* meaning 'skill, method or technique'. The term *artefact* derives from the Latin words *arte factum,* which mean 'made by skill'. In the literal sense, 'art' is something rendered by the skill, method or technique of a human being. 'Art' is a wholly human experience.

3. Deliberate human action

In his book *Art in Action* critic and Christian theologian Nicholas Wolterstorff describes 'art' as 'deliberate human action'. It's worth taking a moment to think about this. 'Deliberate human action' is a very broad definition—some may find it too broad—but there are many liberating possibilities for both professional and amateur artists when we think about art in this way.

The first distinctive is the word 'deliberate'. If art is *deliberate,* anything created by chance or accident is outside the circle. An unintended splash of paint on the wall or the sound of a guitar crashing accidentally to the floor is not art. If, however, we cut the stained wallpaper out and frame it on the wall or record the crashing sound for an album, we would be making art.

Second, if art is 'human' action we can disqualify anything made by animals or found in nature. Paintings made by elephants and the mating calls of parakeets are not art regardless of how skilful they may appear and how melodic or pleasing to the eyes and ears. In the same way we would have to say that trees, sunsets and mountains are outside the circle: the creation is not art and God is not an artist.

The traditional image of God as a celestial painter in the sky would not be strictly accurate. Whilst God is not an artist, this is not to say that he is not creative; far from it. God is the first and absolute Creator with a capital 'C'.

Finally, describing art as an 'action' and not just an object takes art beyond the realm of a mere commodity to be peddled for profit and suggests it is something more profound. The 'work of art' wouldn't be restricted to just a painting on a wall or a sculpture but would also incorporate the actions of the artist in making the art object: their momentum, mark-making and movement as they sculpt. The physical qualities of an art object might be considered a kind of relic or memento of the art action. Cooking a meal, fixing a tyre, digging out weeds, completing a jigsaw, operating on a collapsed lung and preaching a sermon would all be classified as 'art'. By the same criteria, premeditated murder, embezzlement, war, terrorism and other evil activities would also be in the circle. Just because something is 'art' does not necessarily mean it is good.

Whilst some might find 'deliberate human action' too wide a circle or a definition that requires further sub-categorization, it does help us avoid certain red-herring questions such as 'Is it art?' and the annoying wisecrack of the bar-stool critic, 'Anyone could have done that'—to which we can happily reply, 'Yes, anyone can do it, and yes, it is still art!'

'Deliberate human action' frees us to explore more interesting questions such as 'What type of art is it?', 'Is it valuable art?', 'How does the art function?', 'What ideas is the artist exploring?', and the ever tricky 'Is it any good?'

4. Visual signposts to invisible things

Another way of understanding art is as a visible (or physical) object that points towards something that is invisible, such as an idea, a question or a reality we can't see with our eyes. A painting, for example, is more than the accumulation of its physical parts and has the capacity to embody the artist's thoughts, questions and worldviews.

In Psalm 19 we read, 'The heavens declare the glory of God; the skies proclaim the work of his [God's] hands.' Here the psalmist describes how the physical qualities of God's creation—things seen in the skies—

communicate that which is unseen or intangible to the naked eye in God's character: the greatness and glory of the Creator.

When we show our creative side by making a work of art, we echo the creative character of God, and as the visible qualities of his creation point towards the invisible attributes of his character (Rom 1: 20) so the visible qualities of our art communicate something that is invisible to the naked eye. This is the great privilege we share as those made in the image of God.

5. Or simply …

One final way of thinking about art is quite simply 'the stuff we make as artists'. This can be a painting, sculpture, novel, piece of music, play or finely crafted chair. It might even be an idea or concept.

Art might be the things artists make to sell so they can pay the rent. It might be the product of several months' planning, preparing and work. Art might equally be the scrap of paper we doodled on when we were on the phone or the scrap ends of our sketchbook.

The question 'What is art?' leads on to other more personal questions such as 'Why am I making art?', 'Is my art any good?', 'What function does my art have?' and 'What does God think of my art?' These are important questions which we will tackle together over the following chapters.

Take a few moments to think about the nature of art. You might find the following questions helpful:

Q: Which of the above definitions of art resonate with you?

Which don't you like? Why?

3. Is Art a Calling?

(Sketch, doodle, draw. Make this title page your own.)

Every calling is great when greatly pursued.

Oliver Wendall Holmes, American author, wit, poet[8]

A few years ago I met a painting student named Sarah. As a little girl her parents bought her her first set of watercolours and she lost herself in their colours whenever the skies turned grey and clouds lingered over her head. Her skills as an artist developed as she grew older. When she was accepted into her first choice of art college it was the fulfilment of many years' prayer and expectation. At art college Sarah met other artists as passionate as she was about painting. She loved the creative atmosphere but at times felt intimidated by others who just seemed far too talented for their own good! In time she began to question if she really could compete with the high standards expected and doubts started to creep into her mind about whether she could really cut it as an artist in the scary world of life after art college. She had always thought she had a gift for art but now she wasn't sure.

Church life was encouraging and she attended the weekly Bible study that helped her grow in her knowledge of God. In time Sarah began to lead Bible studies at her Christian Union and church home group. She enjoyed opening the Bible with others but always wanted more time to prepare Bible studies well. When her church asked her to apply for a postgraduate apprentice scheme she was flattered but wasn't sure if it was the right thing for her. Should she become an artist or a full-time church worker? One snowy afternoon Sarah asked her Christian Union mates, 'Where do I go from here? What do you think God's calling is for my life?'

Q: What are the issues Sarah faced? How would you counsel her?

Q: How does God guide us today?

When you hear the word 'calling' you might think of moments of profound revelation or booming voices from behind the shaving mirror telling you what to do, but very few of us experience blinding lights or deep voices from the sky saying 'Go forth and become a gra-phic-de-sign-er!'

How then do we know what God wants us to do with our lives? How do we know how best to serve Christ in the arts?

The apostle Paul encouraged his young apprentice, Timothy, to 'fan

8. Oliver Wendell Holmes, 1809–1894. Quoted at BrainyQuote.com (Xplore Inc 2011) on 5 January 2011. http://www.brainyquote.com/quotes/quotes/o/oliverwend378951.html

into flame the gift of God, which is in you' (2 Tim 1:6), and often a sense of purpose comes in our art as we grow in our understanding of God's word and knowledge of our craft. Christ also promised his Spirit to those who follow him so his presence would never leave them. As we are made in the image of God we know that our creative gifts reflect God's own creativity. In a similar way, since God is a moral being, we also know it is a very human experience to make decisions and be responsible for the choices we make. The ability to weigh up different possibilities for a career in the arts and choose what kind of art we want to make is a privilege we share as image bearers of God.

God's word promises, 'If any of you lacks wisdom, he should ask God, who gives generously to all without finding fault, and it will be given to him' (Jas 1:5). We make decisions on a daily basis. Some weigh lightly on our minds, such as what to have for breakfast or where to walk the dog. Other decisions lie more heavily on our minds, such as where to live, whom to live with and what to do with our lives. Since the world is fallen, some decisions will have negative outcomes or not fulfil our best expectations. We will, at times, make the wrong decisions but the Bible promises us that 'in all things

God works for the good of those who love him' (Rom 8:28). Some decisions carry difficult consequences and sacrifices have to be made. Ideals may be compromised, expectations unrealized and things we once held dear may have to be 'put to death'. Sometimes there are personal vanities, egos and foolish or unrealistic dreams that may serve only to harm us and those around us. These also have to be 'put to death'.

When it comes to making art, there are the daily decisions of which colours to use, harmonies to try, words to assemble and materials to invest in, all of which are part of the artist's prerogative to decide. Sometimes decisions are resolved by our intuition because we have trained ourselves to decipher what works best. Most of us will also experience long and fretful days labouring over one piece of work in which every decision we make just seems to make things worse.

The good news is that the Bible clearly states that God will guide his people. God said to the Israelites in exile, 'I know the plans I have for you … plans to prosper you and not to harm you, plans to give you hope and a future' (Jer 29:11). Whilst this was a specific promise to a specific people we can still see God's desires to guide his people and lead them on. In another context, the Psalmist writes, 'the Lord will watch over your coming and going both now and forevermore' (Ps 121:8) and John's gospel also records Jesus' words, 'He calls his own sheep by name and leads them out … his sheep follow him because they know his voice' (John 10:3–4). The biblical picture of God's guidance is one of a caring shepherd who capably leads his sheep and protects them from long-term harm.

God *does* promise to guide his people. Jesus' words in John's gospel describe an eternal guiding, a leading towards the new creation; but God also promises instruction for his people today even though, in practice, it might not feel at all as if we are being led.

What if I make the wrong decision?

Sometimes we can catch ourselves asking, 'What if I make the wrong decision? Is it possible to choose something outside God's will for my life?'

Most of us at some point will ask ourselves if we are really doing what God wants us to do. Does God really want me to be an artist or should I go and do something more 'useful', like being a teacher or church minister?

Throughout the Bible God shows himself to be faithful to his people. He kept the promise he made to Abraham that the Israelite people would become a blessed nation under God's rule and know his protection in the Promised Land, even though they continued to make bad decisions and rebelled against him. We serve a patient God but if we continue to reject his authority God will hand us over to the consequences of our decision against him and cast us out of his presence for eternity (Rom 3:23 and 6:23). It is crucial, however, that we do not confuse consistent disobedience against God with the daily struggles that all Christians face in wrestling sin and living out the complexities of difficult decisions: 'For the Lord will not reject his people; he will never forsake his inheritance' (Ps 94:14). For the Christian, 'If we confess our sins, he is faithful and just and will forgive us our sins and purify us from all unrighteousness' (1 John 1:9).

God will not stop working in our lives just because we made a stupid decision. Even Jonah's disobedience didn't stop the Lord from getting him to where he needed to be. Unless we are actively seeking to disobey the Lord he *will* lead us.

What if there is more than one choice?

There may be a variety of career options we can choose from. When we are faced with many options there might not be a clear distinction between right and wrong. Sometimes instead we need to make a choice between something that is a wise decision over something less wise.

Biblically speaking, there are few jobs we can apply for that are outside God's moral will for our lives. Unless you want to be a lap dancer or porn star (for example), Paul's words still ring true: 'Whatever you do, work at it … as working for the Lord' (Col 3:23). *Whatever* you do—whether you are a vicar, plumber, painter or poet.

The great big snack machine in the sky

When it comes to the bigger decisions of how to serve Christ in the arts, what job to take, which award to apply for, how to manage our time, how to pay the rent and even whom to marry, the answers aren't always easy. Sometimes we catch ourselves wishing that God would give us a sign that would show us without doubt, but then we would miss out on the fundamentally human privilege of choosing one thing from another. To make choices is part of what it means to be human.

Perhaps at other times we can imagine God's guidance as working a bit like a snack machine: we put our prayers in at one end, select the option we prefer and expect God to deliver something wonderful at the other end. The problem comes when we find ourselves with something we didn't order or with nothing at all.

In the book of Psalms God's promise is, 'I will instruct you and teach you in the way you should go' (Ps 32:8). It's a promise echoed in the book of Proverbs:

> Trust in the Lord with all your
> heart
> and lean not on your own
> understanding;
> in all your ways acknowledge
> him,
> and he will make your paths
> straight. (Prov 3:5,6)

On first impression Proverbs 3 seems to suggest that God's guidance will be easy, but what happens when our paths don't seem to be straight? What do we do when we get the Bounty bar instead of the Twix? It can be easy to think that God has given up on us or that we have made a wrong decision. It may well be that we have not been wise in the choices we have made, but God still promises never to leave those who trust in him. Whilst God promises to guide us he never says we will have an easy life. Time and again in the New Testament we are actually instructed to expect the opposite.

Matthew's gospel records Jesus saying, 'If anyone would come after me, he must deny himself and take up his cross and follow me. For whoever wants to save his life will lose it, but whoever loses his life for me will find it' (Matt 16:24,25). Note Jesus' words that those who follow him must deny themselves … pick up their crosses … lose their lives.

Paul also writes to Timothy, 'In fact, everyone who wants to live a godly life in Christ Jesus will be persecuted' (2 Tim 3:12). Paul doesn't say that *some* Christians will have a hard time, but that *all* who follow Christ can expect suffering, persecution and hardship. For us in the arts that may be as tame as a mickey take at

work or not being taken seriously in our art. More seriously, it may involve exclusion from a project or even discrimination by those who are unsympathetic towards our beliefs. I have now heard two art college directors state in their opening addresses to students that their colleges have become atheist communities. In one extreme case an eminent guest lecturer made the public declaration, 'there is no room for religious practice in contemporary art education.'[9] To her credit, during question time at the end of the lecture the leader of the Christian Union raised her hand and said, 'Thank you for your talk. My name is Caroline. I am involved with the Christian group here at the college. We meet every Tuesday night in seminar room D and there is ample room for anyone to come and join us.' What a brilliantly brave and gracious response to an arrogant statement.

God's word never promises that life will be easy, and there will be tough decisions to make. There are times when we disobey God and need to repent. God's word tells us that God disciplines those he loves (Prov 3:12; Heb 12:6) but hardships are often not the result of our sin. God's purpose in our lives is not to make everything easy for us but to make us more like Jesus and ultimately to

9. *From a lecture given by Jonathan Miller to the Royal College of Art, London, 2009.*

lead us into the new creation. As the old hymn puts it,

> Guide me, O Thou great Jehovah,
> Pilgrim through this barren land.
> I am weak, but Thou art mighty;
> Hold me with Thy powerful hand.[10]

Even though it seems at times that life is a barren land we can have confidence in the guiding hand of God who promises to lead those he loves into good things that will display his glory in their lives.

How does it all work out in practice?

How then do we know which decision to make? How does God's guidance work out today in practice? The Bible never promises lightning bolts from the blue but it does give clear instruction for Christians who have decisions to make.

1. Praying for God's help

> Do not be anxious about anything, but in everything, by prayer and petition, with thanksgiving, present your requests to God. (Phil 4:6)

Prayer should be our first priority. If God really is our heavenly Father who is able to do immeasurably more than all we ask or imagine (Eph 3:20), it should be our first instinct to go to him in prayer about everything. Often when we pray we find that God doesn't change the situation around us but instead he changes us, the way we see the problem or our attitude to it.

2. Instruction from God's word

> Your word is a lamp to my feet and a light for my path. (Ps 119:105)

God's word might not tell us which job to do or whom to marry but it does tell us a lot about how we should live, how we should think and how we should work in the arts. God's word was a lamp to the Psalmist's feet, illuminating the way ahead. As a younger Christian I used to approach the Bible as a Magic 8-Ball, asking God my question then opening a page randomly in the hope that an answer would miraculously appear. It wasn't until I asked for God's advice on girls and fell on the words 'have nothing to do with mutilators of the flesh' that I realized that this probably wasn't the most effective way of handling God's word!

10. *William Williams, Bristol, 1745.*

The more we get to know the Bible the more equipped we become in using it when times get tough. Joshua was instructed to meditate on God's word day and night (Josh 1:8). Today when we hear the word 'meditate' we might think of a process of emptying our heads but meditation on the Bible is more about filling our minds with God's words. A great way of doing this is by memorizing verses in the Bible that have become important to you, carrying a Bible around with you through the day and reading it regularly.

3. Keeping perspective

> For the pagans run after all these things, and your heavenly Father knows that you need them. But seek first his kingdom and his righteousness, and all these things will be given to you as well. Therefore do not worry about tomorrow, for tomorrow will worry about itself. Each day has enough trouble of its own. (Matt 6:32–34)

It's important to keep a good perspective on the gravity of a situation. Although it might not feel like it at the time, the big things in life aren't so much about what we should do or even whom we should

marry, but how we live for Christ, how we serve him and are godly in all that we do. This is not to belittle a difficult decision, but it is important that we keep reminding ourselves of the bigger picture.

It might seem important to have a glittering career in the arts with all the fame and fortune it may bring but greater than that is the heavenly reality of God's new creation and our place as citizens in it.

4. Asking for advice from others

> Plans fail for lack of counsel, but with many advisers they succeed. (Prov 15:22)

God has designed us to live in relationship with others. Often he provides good advisors for us at our local churches, and among our friends and families. Sometimes others can help us see things about ourselves that we are not aware of, and those closest to us are able to tell us what our greatest strengths and weaknesses are, if we give them the invitation to do so.

When it comes to what jobs we should take or which commissions we should accept, get advice from those around you whom God has placed in your life to help you make difficult decisions, particularly from those who understand the nature of the creative arts and the issues involved in your decision-making process.

There are several Christian arts groups that may be able to help you in this way such as Morphē (www.morphearts.org), the mentoring project of the Arts Centre Group (www.artscentregroup.org.uk) or Artisan Initiatives (www.artisaninitiatives.org).

5. Using a little common sense

It may sound obvious, but think through the consequences of a potential decision before you make it. If you decide to take a certain job or internship, where will you live? What are the churches like in that area? If it's part-time work, a residency or voluntary, how will you pay the rent? Think about how you cope with big changes and respond to new challenges. What is the best way you can start to make new friends? How can you keep in touch with old friends and other support networks?

It's worth sitting down and thinking through the implications of where your decision will lead. Make a list of pros and cons before making up your mind. Ask as many questions as you can to get a better grasp on what to expect once the decision is made.

So are you 'called' to the arts?

There is a myth that sometimes floats around suggesting that the artist receives something of a higher 'calling' than those in other professions to make extraordinary work. It is the notion of genius: that some people 'have it' while others just don't. Yet most artists I know improve simply because they work hard and have a strong sense that they are doing something valuable and worthwhile. They are passionate about making art and quite simply can't imagine themselves doing anything else.

What is our calling? We are called to be obedient to Christ. Everything else is an outworking of this primary calling.

God gives gifts to all in varying measure. Paul encouraged Timothy to 'fan into flame' the gifts God had given him (2 Tim 1:6). Whilst some may possess a greater gifting for art or something of a 'flair', it is usually those who work hardest for longest who produce the most worthwhile results.

If you have a gift for making art and enjoy it you should look for opportunities to develop your gift as a blessing for others, as gifts are given for communal benefit and not just for individuals. It may be that an opportunity opens for you to study art and work professionally in the arts. If you can and want to, you should take it. It may be that you develop your artistic gift in the context of a local crafts group or even your family. These are all valid uses of a creative gift. I personally pray that all Christians with a gifting in art will strive for excellence in their work and look for opportunities to serve Christ professionally in the arts—but this is a choice, not a mandate (although what a great choice it is!).

If you're considering a career in the arts you probably won't be doing it for the money, so it's worth visualizing what that might look like for you in years to come. How will you sustain a living? How will you live after art college? What art will you make? Where will you make it?

The question of what art you will make is best answered by simply making work. As artists we think as we make, rather than resolving the issues before the pencil has even scratched the paper. As a Christian you are free to make art on any subject and in any medium. As a helpful starting point, think about what interests you. What work has been successful in the past for you? What do others think you're good at? What art do you enjoy seeing, hearing or reading? These are the obvious questions but it's often the elementary ideas that bear the richest fruit.

Q: What decisions do you face at the moment? How can you ask for God's help?

Q: Whom do you need to talk to before making your decision? What other help do you need and where can you get it?

Take a few moments to thank God for the creative gifts he has given you, and ask for his help in fanning these gifts into flame. Ask that he might open opportunities for your art. Ask that you might have the courage to take the opportunities when they come.

4. How is Art Worship?

(Sketch, doodle, draw. Make this title page your own.)

Whatever you do, work at it with all your heart, as working for the Lord, not for men.

Colossians 3:23

Therefore, I urge you, brothers, in view of God's mercy, to offer your bodies as living sacrifices, holy and pleasing to God—this is your spiritual act of worship.

Romans 12:1

At Camberwell School of Art in 2010, Christian students wrote a questionnaire for their course mates as a way of raising issues of art and faith. The first question asked, 'Why do you make art?' The most popular response was 'to express myself'. The second question asked, 'Whom do you make art for?' to which the most popular reply was, 'I make it for myself'. Imagine you were filling in the questionnaire. What answers would you give?

Q: Why do you make art?

Q: Whom do you make art for?

In years gone by there was a tradition that Christian writers would use the initials S.D.G. at the opening of their books as a form of dedication. S.D.G. is an abbreviation of the Latin phrase *Soli Deo Gloria,*

which means 'for the sole glory of God', leaving no room to doubt why they were making art and whom they primarily aspired to make work for.

Q: Imagine the letters S.D.G. stencilled on the back of your canvas or as the screensaver on your Mac or PC. How would it affect your creative practice?

Soli Deo Gloria

The Westminster Confession of Faith states, 'The chief end of man is to glorify God.' In a previous chapter we considered art as an action or experience that is essentially human. If art is an action perhaps we could also make sense of the Confession of Faith by saying, 'The chief end of art is to glorify God.'

This chapter is all about worship. What does it mean to be an artist and a worshipper of Jesus Christ? Aside from the writing of hymns and other forms of creativity used in church services, how can the everyday practices of art-making outside the walls of church bring glory to God?

In the Bible the word 'worship' is a translation of three different words which suggest slightly different aspects of worship. The Greek word *proskuneo* means 'to show homage or submission'. It suggests a physical act of worship: to bow down or lie prostrate on the ground, as demonstrated by the two Marys who bowed down on encountering the risen Christ in the garden (Matt 28:9).

The Greek word *phobeomai* translates as 'to revere' or 'to fear'. The apostle Paul writes much about fearing the Lord; in 2 Corinthians 5:11 he states, 'Since, then, we know what it is to fear the Lord, we try to persuade men.' To revere and fear the Lord is an act of worship.

The third word, *latreuo,* means 'to serve'. We see this kind of worship recorded in Exodus when God speaks to Moses through the burning bush and promises that Israel will 'worship God on this mountain' (Exod 3:12). Later Moses is sent to tell Pharaoh to release God's people in slavery so they might worship the Lord instead of serving their Egyptian slave-masters (Exod 8:1).

Serving the Lord is more than a best intention or positive way of thinking; it involves the whole of our minds, bodies and actions. It requires all that we think, say and do as an act of spiritual sacrifice. 'Therefore, I urge you, brothers, in view of God's mercy, to offer your bodies as living sacrifices, holy and pleasing to God— this is your spiritual act of worship [*latreuo*]' (Rom 12:1,2). Our spiritual act of service is to offer everything we have and all that we are as a living sacrifice to God, including our artistic practice. What does it mean to serve the Lord in our art? How can we offer ourselves as living sacrifices to God in the professional creative industries?

Art and excellence

When God created the world he declared that it was 'good'. We know that the creation itself declares the glory of God (Ps 19:1), the quality of God's work speaking for itself.

Since we are made in the image of God it is right to aspire to be good at what we do, not for our own sakes but that the praise might go to God; the apostle Matthew recorded Jesus' words in another context, 'that they may see your good deeds and praise your Father in heaven' (Matt 5:16). The question is, how do we make art for the glory of God? What does that look like?

As we look at those in the Bible whom God gifted in art and was pleased with, it was often the excellent quality of their work that delighted the Lord, as well as their characters and godly lives. The art of Bezalel in Exodus 31 was technically exceptional; David's songs, Solomon's poetry and the apostle John's prose (to name just a few) were also magnificent works of art in their own right. As we have seen already, Paul writes, 'Whatever you do, work at it with all your heart, as working for the Lord, not for men' (Col 3:23) but he also writes, 'Make it your ambition to lead a quiet life, to mind your own business and to work with your hands, just as we told you' (1 Thess 4:11). It seems that simply getting on with the work is viewed as a godly working method by God's word.

How then do we work with all our hearts for the Lord in our art? Perhaps, at first, it quite simply means that we are to work hard: to graft, practise, focus, mature, develop and strive.

A defining moment in Michael Parkinson's career came during his TV interview with Pablo Picasso shortly before the latter's death in 1973. Recognizing the great painter's age Parkinson took the opportunity to commission an original drawing live on air. Picasso accepted and took two minutes to sketch Parkinson's portrait as the interview continued. Parkinson was thrilled. It was an excellent sketch. Out of interest he asked Picasso how much the sketch was worth, to which Picasso wryly replied that it would probably fetch around six thousand pounds. Parkinson exclaimed, surprised that something achieved in such a short time could possibly be worth so much. But Picasso, easing back into his armchair, was completely unfazed. That drawing had not been achieved in just two minutes, he explained, for he had been working on that drawing his entire life.

Picasso knew, as all true masters know, that greatness takes time to mature.

Art and character

As those who work in the creative industries as professional artists it is really important that we pursue artistic excellence. When Bezalel crafted the artefacts for the tabernacle his technical skill was the finest in the land. God was interested in his ability but he was also interested in the excellence of his character. The way we create matters to God as much as the substance of what we create.

God takes interest in art made by professionals and amateurs alike. Psalm 149 commemorates a great battle won by God for the nation of Israel. In praise, the Israelites perform music for their Lord as they sing, dance and generally make a raucous noise to say thanks to God. They even dance on their beds! Take a moment to imagine the Israelites celebrating that night. Among them, no doubt, would have been a few accomplished musicians but the majority would have been average Joes wanting to sing their hearts out to God. They probably looked and sounded a bit like we all do at church on a Sunday morning (or even more like those at a gig or club on a Saturday night!). This was not a professional concert yet God was 'delighted' with their creative offering.

Christians are to strive for excellence in their art but we are not called to perfection. For some that means rehearsing hard once a week for the church music group or planning an art lesson well for kids. For others it means study and practice for the rest of our lives.

God gives generously to all, but since 'We have different gifts, according to the grace given us' (Rom 12:6) we are to work with all our hearts as working for the Lord, whether we are highly skilled or budding amateurs.

Self-expression and godly communication

At Camberwell School of Art, the majority of students who were asked why they made art said they did it as a form of self-expression. What exactly do we express when we express ourselves?

As Christians we believe that the Holy Spirit dwells within us and therefore when we express ourselves we are expressing something of Christ in us. The problem is that at the same time there is much of my old self that continues to fester within me even as the Spirit does his sanctifying work. Therefore, when I express myself I will also be expressing something of my sin.

Christians have died to self in order to live for Christ. Surely our motivation for art-making must move beyond self-referential demonstrations and mere self-expression? This is not to say that we shouldn't make art about ourselves or draw from our personal experiences to inform our work (the psalmist David refers to himself much of the time) but our goal ultimately is to point to Christ, not ourselves.

In a recent TV documentary, the senior tutor at Goldsmiths Art College, London, described art as 'an argument or proposal of a position that's being put forward to the world'.[11] Art may be a form of self-expression but it is also a communication to others. Every artist has an audience, even if that audience is only of one. When we express ourselves we have no need to relate to others, but when we communicate it is deeply important for us to know whom we are communicating to. Who is our audience? How do they think? What languages do they speak, whether visual or audible? The apostle Paul writes, 'Do nothing out of selfish ambition or vain conceit but in humility consider others better than yourselves. Each of you should look not only to you own interests, but also to the interests of others' (Phil 2:3,4).

When we consider art as a relational activity we echo the character of God who created us so that creation might recognize his greatness (Ps 19; Rom 1). His creation was a form of self-expression but it was also a communication of how great God is. In this sense, when we create our art can be worship to God when it is made well and communicates something of God's glory and his desires for a broken world.

Q: What are your priorities as a Christian? How do your expectations and ambitions as an artist relate to these priorities?

Q: What will it look like for you to worship God in your studio, rehearsal room or study this week?

11. *From the BBC documentary* Goldsmiths: But Is It Art? *(BBC 3, April 2009).*

5. What Good is Art?

(Sketch, doodle, draw. Make this title page your own.)

*Works of art equip us for
action. And the range of
actions for which they equip
us is very nearly as broad as
the range of human action
itself. The purposes of art
are the purposes of life. To
envisage human existence
without art is not to envisage
human existence. Art—so often
thought of as a way of getting
out of the world—is man's way
of acting in the world.*

Nicholas Wolterstorff, Christian theologian
and writer[12]

*Artworks should engage,
articulate, problematise, open
new ways of seeing, place the
viewer in jeopardy of their
received opinions, move the
artists to the limits of what they
know or believe, excite, incite,
entertain, annoy, get under
the skin and when you've done
with them, nag at your mind to
go take another look.*

Mark Wallinger, contemporary artist[13]

If I'm introduced to somebody at
a party and they ask, 'So what do
you do?' and I say, 'I'm an artist',
pretty much a wall goes up straight
away. It might be that there's a little
bit of envy but I wonder if they're
really thinking, 'Oh, so you're out
there skipping through fields and

12. *From the
first chapter of
his book* Art in
Action: Toward
a Christian
Aesthetic *(Grand
Rapids, MI:
Eerdmans, 1980 /
Carlisle: Paternos-
ter, 2000), p. 4.*

13. *From an article
reproduced in*
Art for All: Their
Policies and Our
Culture *(London:
Peer, 1998), p.
133.*

picking flowers and probably just
navel-gazing all day, and not being a
productive member of society.'

Q: What do your friends, family
and church mates think of you
being an artist?

Q: Why do you think art is not
always seen as a valid career
choice?

So why become an artist? The idea
that Christian mission and art are
somehow mutually exclusive is
definitely not biblical. The Bible is
full of those who made art for the
glory of God and received God's
blessing, something we will explore
further in the next part of this book.

Even so, there can sometimes
be a sense that art is a bit of an
unnecessary indulgence or is
somehow less useful to society than
other vocations, such as becoming a
doctor, teacher, church minister or
even pet psychologist.

When God created the world, before
he said that the trees were 'good
for food' he said that they were
'pleasing to the eye' (Gen 2:9). We
can see that God takes pleasure in
how his creation looks as well as in
how it functions. This helps us to see
that art doesn't need to 'say' or 'do'

anything in order to be pleasing to the Lord; it can simply be art.

Sometimes there's a sense that we should go into art out of a sense of duty, seeing art as a tool for evangelism or an avenue to influence those who have a greater influence on society. It's true that the arts are an undeniable factor in shaping how we live and think. We need to take this responsibility seriously, but at the same time not imagine that we will all get to make art on a national platform or meet the prime minister. Most of us will be making art in local communities or teaching and making art at regional galleries or schools. We don't need to enter the arts out of an unrealistic pressure to change the world. Rather we make art quite simply because we love it and are grateful to the God who has given us the gifts and desires to make art well.

What then are the ways in which art can do some good in the world? Here are a few ideas. What do you think?

Art as a blessing

Genesis 1:28 records how God blessed Adam and Eve; in return they were instructed to lead fruitful lives and to increase in number. In Genesis 9:1 a similar instruction is given to Noah. As God gave blessing to his people, so they were instructed by God to bear fruit and bring increase to the world. In this early sense, to bless someone was to bring increase and enlargement to them.

Art can be a blessing when it enlarges the imaginations, reason, sensibilities and actions of others. To bless culture is to enlarge it. When Christians enter the artistic arena it really should be good news for creative culture. As Bezalel sculpted the artefacts for the tabernacle the Israelites were blessed with sensory symbols in sight, sound, touch and smell that enlarged their devotion to God.

Art can bring a blessing, but the blessing may not always feel good. When Jacob received a blessing from the Lord he walked away with a limp. When the disciples were blessed with an invitation to follow Christ they could not have known the hardships and persecutions this new life would bring them. When we are confronted with the truth there is no guarantee that it will make us feel good or that we will even like what we hear.

Just because something feels bad it does not mean that we have not been blessed. Recently I saw Steven

Spielberg's *Schindler's List* again. I couldn't say that I enjoyed the film or that it made me feel good, but it certainly enlarged my awareness of this dark period in human history and the brutal realities of war.

The blessing of art can be painful for the audience but it may also be painful for the artist. When my aunt visited me on the eve of my degree show she walked right past me in the corridor, not recognizing my undernourished, sleep-deprived and generally emaciated frame! I had worked hard for that degree show, perhaps too hard, and had suffered the consequences. But not all art processes lead to washed-out artists. Art should invigorate, restore and refresh the artist, not lead them to exhaustion. When we make art we perform a fundamentally human activity that was intended for us by God and that therefore is good, bringing enlargement to our understanding and enjoyment of God, his creation or ourselves. Yet art, like all other aspects of creation, has become subject to the fall and so what once was good is now frustrated. When Christian philosopher Calvin Seerveld wrote to encourage Christian artists he instructed them:

> You cannot bludgeon people with Christian art into accepting Jesus Christ. But neither should you settle for being as dispassionately good as the secular professional artist, adding: 'I do it for Jesus you know.' It is the crux of your task as a communal body of fellow Christian artists to fire your art until it emits sparks that warm, or burn, those it reaches.[14]

Art as a curse

Just because something feels bad it does not mean it is not a blessing. On the other hand, just because something feels good there is no guarantee that it is actually doing us good. Art can perform a blessing but it can also be a curse. Just as *blessing* in the Bible brought increase, so a *curse* brought reduction. In Genesis 3, the snake was reduced to being the lowest of all livestock and to crawling on its belly after it tricked Adam and Eve into rebelling against God. In the same way, the earth itself was cursed, becoming harder to work and bearing less fruit as a result of the fall. To curse someone is to reduce them in some way.

As a Scot, I'm a big fan of deep-fried Mars Bars. There's nothing as sweet as the oozing hot caramel seeping

14. *From the second chapter of Calvin Seerveld,* Bearing Fresh Olive Leaves *(Carlisle: Piquant, 2000), p. 35.*

through the batter and glazing your taste buds (not to mention your shirt!). It's the extreme-sports version of late-night snackery. Everybody knows that deep-fried Mars Bars are bad for you, but they certainly make you feel great, at least in a lardy/sugar rush sort of way. Sometimes art can be a bit like a deep-fried Mars Bar. The initial sensation may be sweet but the long-term effects are far from healthy. Mars Bars enlarge your waistline but that is the only long-term 'blessing' they bring on a person. In the same way, art can make you feel really great in the short term but do nothing for your spiritual health in the long term.

Kitsch art makes many people feel great. A picture of a romanticized sunset or an overly cute puppy appeals to the sentiments but does nothing for our understanding of reality. This is art tailored to the escapist sensibilities of the viewer rather than to an understanding of the world as it really is. Kitsch art doesn't open the eyes of its audience to new ideas or enhance our understanding of God's world. Rather it panders to the familiar and anesthetizes the imagination. In the same way, a blockbuster movie that pulls out all the stops on the effects and music can sometimes take us

for an emotional ride just for the sake of it and reduce or curse rather than bless or enlarge us. Art that offers mere sentiment, insincerity or manipulation, art that panders to popular ideals, art that anaesthetizes the imagination, art that sugar-coats reality or reduces the truth is a curse to us.

Art as a relationship (not a commodity)

Before there was creation there was a relationship within the Godhead. As those made in the image of God we are to be relational as we create. If art is born out of the relational character of a creative God so we, as artists, should be primarily focused on bringing blessing to others through relationship.

An art object can enlarge our understanding of the world and of the way we see reality through our own eyes and through the eyes of the artist, and it can change the way we live, but the real value of a work of art exceeds the limitations of a price tag or the sum value of its physical parts. Art is not just a commodity but a way of seeing, a means to enter into a dialogue with those it reaches.

Skip Schuckmann is a contemporary visual artist who works with local communities, such as villages, schools or indigenous communities, in North America. Since he focuses more on the creative process between artist and client he prevents his work becoming a commodity, avoiding the restrictions of commercial art markets. His clients don't buy his work; instead they enter into a relationship with the artist who sees himself as an educator or teacher rather than an initiator of public artworks or purveyor: 'I am a mentor and orchestrator in the development of people's physical and mental properties.'[15]

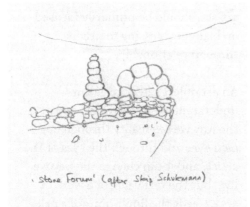

' Stone Forum' (after Skip Schuckmann)

15. *In an interview with Linda Wein-traub in* Making Contemporary Art: How Today's Artists Think and Work *(London: Thames and Hudson, 2003), p. 34.*

Schuckmann offers one-on-one tutorials in art-making so that his clients can participate in the making as much as the artist himself. He prefers non-precious materials such as wood, earth and rocks, making art that reaches way beyond the walls of any gallery by conventional standards, choosing instead the great outdoors; his studio can literally be anywhere. Schuckmann is a man of routine. Every day he orders the same meal from Antonio's Mexican Cafe in Ojai, California. This daily ritual symbolizes, for him, the beauty of the mundane; he loves the normal, the boring, and the everyday, and forces the recipients of his artworks to slow down their pace of life and enjoy the simplicity of nature.

Art as a window

One traditional function of art is to serve as a window to see the beauty and grandeur of the natural world. In this way art can help us experience the world as seen through the eyes of the artist. We might see something of God's character that we hadn't realized before or that can't be expressed in word alone.

In Caspar David Friedrich's epic Romantic painting *Wanderer above the Mists,* for example, viewers are encouraged to place themselves where the artist places the central figure, looking out from a rocky outcrop towards the sublime expanse of the landscape before him. Since the figure has turned his back to us we are less occupied with what he looks like and encouraged instead to cast our gaze out to the mountains and mist beyond. The figure may even be the artist himself. As such the painting acts as a window through which we quite literally see what the artist remembers of the view from high above.

The Wanderer (after Friedrich)

When we consider art made by others it can open a new way of seeing for us, exploring a new idea, philosophy or opinion that may be different from our own. In this way art can be a great vehicle for understanding both the beauty of the created world and the fallen nature of the world. Art can be a window both to show something of God's creation but also to view the culture in which God has placed us. As artists seek to explore the ideas that inform the way we think as individuals and communities, their art can help us better understand the world we Christians hope to reach with the good news of Christ.

Art as a mirror

In a similar way art can function as a mirror to reflect the ideas and values of the world. If we want to find out what the world is thinking, art can be a good starting point.

Jeremy Deller makes art on a range of subjects including the politics and histories of communities on the fringes of mainstream culture. Deller was winner of the Turner Prize in 2004. His show at Tate Britain included an installation titled *Memory Bucket,* a documentary about Crawford, Texas—the hometown of President George W. Bush—and the siege in nearby Waco. He has also made art about the miners' strikes of the 1980s in northern England and their lasting impact on local people.

Much of Deller's work is collaborative. His *Folk Archive,* for example, is a tour of 'people's art' outside of the contemporary art institution and showcases art made by local people about local events.

In many ways we could say that Deller's art functions as a mouthpiece for the communities he makes art about. But it does more than that. Deller's art examines the processes that make culture itself. He examines the events and histories that shape the lives of individuals and communities. In so doing we might say that his work functions as a mirror that reflects both the ideas of the artist and the circumstances of the people he makes art about.

Art as a point of contact

Art can also function by building bridges between people from different backgrounds; between us who would call ourselves Christian and those who don't share our deepest beliefs. Art can be a mutual talking point or a catalyst for valuable conversations: a way of mutually enjoying the world or questioning it together.

Some of the most engaging conversations I have enjoyed with art students I have worked with over the years have begun with the simple

question, 'Can you tell me about your art?' Most artists appreciate an opportunity to talk about their work. We make art in the hope that others will discuss and enjoy it together.

Nathan Coley is a contemporary Scottish installation artist who makes sculptural installations based on architectural themes and the institutions of religious belief. He was nominated for the Turner Prize in 2007 for his large cardboard sculptures of a synagogue, mosque and church.

* there will be no miracles here (after Nathan Coley)*

His installation *There Will Be No Miracles Here* was inspired by a seventeenth-century story from the French village of Modseine. The village was apparently the site of a Christian revival and various miracles and conversions were reported. The local authorities took umbrage at this and eventually a notice was put up stating, 'There will be no miracles here, by order of the King.' Coley's installation recreates the king's edict in bright lights fastened to a large steel frame, reminiscent of billboard advertising or the neon glow of theatre and cinema billings.

There is much that Christians can discuss in Nathan Coley's art, which is common ground for the asking of important questions and raising of difficult issues. Here art may serve as a connecting point for open debate and mutual consideration between Christians and those who may be interested in the themes of communicating faith, belief and even miracles.

Art as a hammer

The creative arts are a powerful force for shaping the ideas and culture of society. Think about how many novels you have read in the last year, how many images you have seen, how many magazines you have read or how many films you have watched. According to one national newspaper cinema attendance on a Saturday evening is fifteen times greater than church attendance on a Sunday in the UK.

It's interesting to think how many political campaigns over the last couple of decades have been spearheaded by artists. We might think of the Jubilee 2000 campaign, Make Poverty History, Live Aid, Band Aid or the Stop the War Coalition, each of which have not been led by politicians (or even clergy, for that matter) but by musicians, artists and TV presenters. The creative arts are influencing us; the question is, who is influencing the creative arts?

In the Genesis story God puts Adam to work in the Garden of Eden 'to work it and take care of it' (Gen 2:15). This mandate to work in God's creation and take care of it continues today. As artists we must play our part in stewarding culture with the artistic tools God has placed at our fingertips. He also instructed Adam and Eve to 'Be fruitful and increase in number; fill the earth and subdue it' (Gen 1:28). The art that we make must bring a blessing, bear fruit and enlarge culture, and these are issues we will discuss in more detail in the next chapter.

Whilst a hammer is a neutral object, in the hands of a skilful craftsman it can be used to build something good; but a hammer can also be employed to demolish. In the same way the creative arts and media may be used as tools for building, but they can also demolish that which is good and godly.

Art as a worldview or polemic

Not all forms of cultural demolition are a curse, as the apostle Paul writes: 'The weapons we fight with are not the weapons of the world ... We demolish arguments and every pretension that sets itself up against the knowledge of Christ, and we take captive every thought to make it obedient to Christ' (2 Cor 10:4,5).

Just as a work of art can initiate a dialogue so it can also present to its audience a way of viewing the world that reflects the character of God, his plans for the creation or the fallen nature of the world. A work of art can make an argument, ask a question, get under the skin and rattle a few cages. As the weapons we fight with are not of this world we have the advantage through prayer and application of God's word to make the best kind of art that not only reflects the beauty of God's world and excellence of its design but also demonstrates its need for a saviour, even serving as a signpost to the solution found in Christ. Our art should be authentic in a world of fakery as it reflects the truth of God's reality and even points towards a greater reality to come.

Q: Think about each of these possible functions for art. How does your art function in these ways? Are there other ways your art can bring a blessing to the world?

Q: How else can art bless or curse those it reaches?

Q: Jesus said, 'let your light shine before men, that they may see your good deeds and praise your Father in heaven' (Matt 5:16). How can art function as a 'good deed'?
How can your art lead others to praise your Father in heaven?

6. How Does Art Function in the Kingdom of God?

(Sketch, doodle, draw. Make this title page your own.)

The time has come ... The kingdom of God is near. Repent and believe the good news!'

Mark 1:15

The earth is the Lord's, and everything in it.

Psalm 24:1

Jesus talked a lot about the Kingdom of God, using parables and stories to describe it to his followers, but before we ask how art functions in God's Kingdom we first need to work out what we mean by 'Kingdom of God'. When we pray 'thy kingdom come' what exactly do we mean? How does God's Kingdom come in the creative arts and media?

Q: What is the Kingdom of God?

Q: Jesus said that the Kingdom of God is like a field, pearl, net and a mustard seed. What do you think he meant? Doodle, draw, sketch. You know what to do.

- field (Matt 13:24–29,36–42)
- hidden treasure and pearl (Matt 13:44,45)
- net (Matt 13:47–52)
- mustard see and yeast (Matt 13:31-34)

We talk a lot about the Kingdom of God but have you ever stopped to think about what, where, when and who is in this Kingdom, let alone how to make art for it and in it?

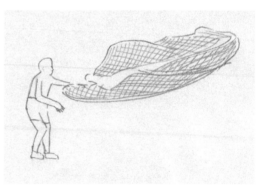

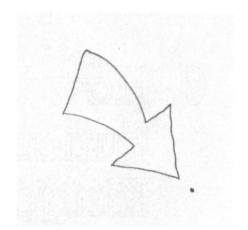

The people of the Kingdom

The Kingdom of God is referred to throughout the Bible as the place of God's authority and rule. The people of the Kingdom are those who worship God and are bound by his covenantal love for them. In the Garden of Eden, God's people were Adam and Eve. After the fall it was the Israelites. Since the Israelites continued to rebel against the Lord, God promised to set up a new people and nation whose hearts would be changed. In the New Testament much points toward this new 'nation' being revealed in Jesus. Today, those who are 'in Christ' are part of his nation and have become the new people of God's Kingdom.

The location of the Kingdom

Jesus said, 'My kingdom is not of this world ... my kingdom is from another place' (John 18:36). He also said, 'The kingdom of God is near' (Mark 1:15), 'the kingdom of God has come upon you' (Matt 12:28) and 'the kingdom of God is within you' (Luke 17:21). So where exactly is it?

In the Old Testament, the Kingdom of God was first established in the Garden of Eden. Later, God dwelt amongst his people through the tabernacle and temple of the Israelites. In the opening chapter of John, the gospel writer says that Jesus 'made his dwelling among us' as God in human flesh—quite literally this means he 'pitched his tent' (or tabernacled) with his people. God's Kingdom was located in Jesus. Today, since the Spirit of Christ dwells in those who follow him, the Kingdom of God is located in the lives, actions and (dare we say it?) art of Christians.

The rule of the Kingdom

Every Kingdom has a king and the sovereign of God's Kingdom is Jesus Christ. In Colossians 1, Paul writes, 'all things were created by him [Jesus] and for him ... He is the head ... so that in everything he might have the supremacy.' Jesus is the author and inventor of all things and everything belongs to him, including the creative arts and media: 'he is the ... firstborn from among the dead, so that in everything he might have the supremacy. For God was pleased to have all his fulness dwell in him' (Col 1:18–19). Since Jesus is author and inventor of the arts he can do whatever he pleases with them. Therefore, when we pray 'thy kingdom come' in the arts we are recognizing Christ's sovereign rule over creative culture and asking him to show his authority over them.

The 'now and not yet' of the Kingdom

In the future Jesus will return to establish his rule over a new heaven and new earth. As Christians we look forward to the future kingdom of God where 'There will be no more death or mourning or crying or pain, for the old order of things has passed away' (Rev 21:4). We will live with Christ and there will be new art, renewed love and much to look forward to.

The 'new creation' isn't just a future event. Paul says in 2 Corinthians 5, 'if anyone is in Christ, he is a new creation; the old has gone, the new has come', meaning that for those who are in Christ there is the possibility of new life now. There can be new art, new hope and new passion for Jesus today in our own lives as well as in the creative arts. As Christians we live in the tension between the 'now' of living by faith today and the 'not yet' of knowing the full reality of the Kingdom in the future. (We'll discuss these ideas further in chapter 12.)

The gospel of the Kingdom—Jesus is Lord!

Jesus said, 'The time has come. The kingdom of God is near. Repent and believe the good news!' (Mark 1:15). Since the word 'gospel' means 'good news' we know that Jesus' call to repentance was a call to believe the gospel of God's Kingdom. Many of the New Testament writers expand on this connection; for example, the apostle Matthew describes the gospel itself as 'the good news of the kingdom' (Matt 4:23; 9:35; 24:14).

So what is the gospel? The gospel of God's Kingdom is the 'good news' that Jesus is Lord and Saviour: it's the good news that Jesus is Lord over everything. So when we ask, 'How does art function in the Kingdom of God?' we are also asking, 'How does art give glory to Jesus?' or even 'How does art demonstrate the Lordship of Christ?'

When we talk about the gospel we might be tempted to begin by talking about ourselves: what Jesus has done for *us* and how *we* have been saved. Whilst this is part of the gospel and, of course, a wonderful truth the reality of the matter is that the starting point of the gospel is not us but the Lordship of Jesus Christ himself. When Peter stood up to preach the gospel at Pentecost he was quick to divert attention away from what God had done for the apostles through the Holy Spirit and chose instead to talk about the facts concerning Jesus Christ. The gospel is all about Jesus: his glory, his rule and his Lordship over all things. When we ask how art functions in the Kingdom of God the answer is quite simple: to glorify Jesus Christ. The big question is, what does this look like in practice?

Q: How do the Lordship and salvation of Jesus Christ shape your art practice?

Q: How does *your* art function in the Kingdom of God?

As a young artist trying to relate my faith to my art I was disappointed by the apparent lack of places to turn. I'd never heard Bible teaching on the arts and there seemed to be very few Christians around who could help me understand the role of God's Spirit in making art today. Then a friend introduced me to Steve Turner's book *Imagine* and it was like a breeze of fresh air on a muggy day. Turner wrote about how much God values the aesthetic qualities of art, and how he doesn't just want guitar-led church bands and altar painters but Christians

working in every level of society and the arts. Turner was a Christian who talked about cool things like albums, paintings and films. He seemed to be into the kind of stuff I loved as an artist, not just using them as sermon-illustration fodder. He talked about how Christian culture, in particular evangelical, had evolved away from the arts through centuries of misunderstandings and lack of interest in art and was only now starting to wake up to the possibilities of having a Christian voice in the creative industries again: 'Evangelical Christians have traditionally taken redemption as their starting point to anything. Had the artist been reborn and was the artist singing, writing or painting about being reborn? ... Christians had often diminished the importance of human endeavour in the arts, and in doing this had deprived themselves of a wealth of cultural experience.'[16]

Today, I believe, Christians are better equipped than ever for engaging professionally with the creative arts. We are indebted to the new writing of Steve Turner, Calvin Seerveld, Hilary Brand, Adrienne Chaplin, Makoto Fujimura, Jeremy Begbie, Tim Keller and many others, as well as older writers such as Francis Schaeffer, Hans Rookmaaker and C.

16. Imagine: A Vision for Christians in the Arts *(Nottingham: IVP, 2001), p. 12.*

S. Lewis. There are blogs, websites and artists' journals dedicated to the interface between Christian faith and contemporary art and there is still room for more Christian critical enquiry into the arts today.

However, artists are foremost makers of art. And in making art Christians are not exempt from having to grapple with the human realities that are revealed throughout the redemptive history recorded in the Bible: we too are *created* and *fallen*.

> For although they knew God, they neither glorified him as God nor gave thanks to him. (Rom 1:21)

The Adoration of the Golden Calf (after Nicholas Poussin)

But we, too, have been *redeemed*. And in the book of Revelation we are shown a glimpse into the future. There, musicians and artists herald in the New Jerusalem, where there

will be music, dance, architecture, buildings, food, wine—a full diversity of culture even richer than that in this first creation. At the centre of this new creation will be Jesus Christ, who sits enthroned as Lord and Saviour of everything.

The themes of creation, fall and redemption will be discussed again, and more fully, in chapters 8 to 12.

Q: Where do you see a demonstration of creation, fall, redemption and recreation in the creative arts today?

Q: How can 'thy kingdom come' be evident in your own creative practice?

7. What is the Artist's Task Today

(Sketch, doodle, draw. Make this title page your own.)

*Mankind is called to develop
this world, to work in it in the
fields of art, science, politics
and economics. Christians
should not withdraw from any
of these fields. They should
be active in all these areas,
because they are a part of
God's creation and God is
more deeply present in all His
work than we ever imagined.*[17]

Wim Rietkerk, writer and tutor at L'Abri
Christian Fellowship

*The message of responsible
social transformation is the
artistic concept. Wherever
there is this concept, there is
art.*[18]

Michelangelo Pistoletto, art critic and artist

Every generation of artists has its
problems to solve. We each have
unique challenges to overcome and
ideas to respond to depending on
the Zeitgeist and the creative-culture
arena in which God has placed us.

Q: What questions raised on your
course or amongst your peers
connect with your faith in Christ?

Q: What issues in contemporary
culture cause dispute over belief
in Christ?

The function of the arts and the role
of the artist in society has changed
over the years. When we read of
the arts in the Old Testament, for
example, it is clear that they fulfilled
a particular task but one that is
different in many ways from how the
arts function today.

Bezalel and his team of craftsmen
were commissioned to construct the
artefacts for the tabernacle, working
to the blueprints God had given to
Moses. Whilst there are similarities
here with the design industries today,
Bezalel's task was quite different from
ours if we work in the mainstream
arts today. Perhaps it is more helpful
to compare our situation with that of
Paul at Mars Hill (Acts 17); there he
responded with a positively Christian
worldview to the issues that were
being raised by the art of the time.

When I first started a job as art staff
worker for UCCF: The Christian
Unions I met a group of art students
who were just starting to think
through how their faith related to
their art. I asked them what they
imagined to be the best opportunity
they might have to serve Christ in
the arts. They said that it would be
to exhibit work at a major Christian
conference, such as Spring Harvest or
Soul Survivor. As much as I wanted
to encourage involvement with these

17. The Future
Great Planet
Earth (Good-
books, 1989).
Currently out of
print.

18. From an article
on Arte Povera,
Art Review, Sep-
tember 2008.

events I couldn't help but feel a little sad at the limitations of this vision. Jesus said that we are the salt and light of the world (Matt 5:13,14). We are to shine our light before men. We are to be active in society. We are to be in culture and encultured, although not subject to its demands, ideologies and fashions. We must avoid making art in a Christian bubble or hiding behind some kind of ivory-tower theology that has no practical application for the real world.

The role of the artist in the past

Artists were viewed in various ways in the past: as anonymous craftsmen or specialized tradesmen before the Renaissance, or as Romantics, bohemians, prophets and priests thereafter. At certain times we have been regarded merely as entertainers; at others, eccentric geniuses or even gurus, mystics and priests, bringing hope and inspiration to the people. In the early twentieth century the notion of the avant-garde presented the artist as a visionary and pioneer. Artists became elitists, celebrities, even role models to aspire towards—a far cry from the artisans of old whose social standing was no greater than that of the local plumber, carpenter or cook.

... guru
... faceless artisan
... craftsmen
... Romantic
... prophet
... elite
... entertainer
... all of the above?
... none of the above?

What do you think?

In many ways the role of the artist relates to the needs of the world around them. We might therefore ask, what are the needs of society today and how can we Christians use art as a vehicle to minister to those needs? Never before have the arts been so well positioned to influence wider society as they are today. With more students enrolling in creative arts courses and government funding for the arts being at an all-time high, our generation enjoys privileges and responsibilities never before experienced. What shall we do with such advantages? Here are a few thoughts.

Artists can …

… Help others see and listen

The role of the artist in opening a window into new realities for the viewer has never been more apparent. In an increasingly visual culture we can help others see something of God's design for his creation, something of the fallen nature of the world and something of our unique way of seeing these issues as Christians.

When we look at a piece of visual art we enter into a multisensory experience in which we listen with our eyes. What are we listening to? Simply put, we listen to the voice of the artist: her questions, ideas and worldview; his arguments, polemic

and statements. In some ways, looking at and listening to a painting is a bit like starting a conversation with the artist or continuing a dialogue that is already open. The arts have a wonderful ability to open discussion beyond the limits of other forms of communication.

As artists we need to listen to the voices that shape the world around us. We listen so that we might respond relevantly to what we hear.

… Explore the truth

Ellis Potter is a regular speaker at our Interface Arts events. He once described the role of the artist: 'We know objectively and subjectively and there is accurate and non-accurate truth. We build bridges accurately and truly but we fall in love non-accurately and truly. Science helps us to know truth objectively and accurately while art helps us to know truth subjectively and non-accurately.'[19]

Art can explore true events within the world as we see it in a way that the sciences cannot. Ellis uses the example of love. It is a matter of fact that I love my wife but I cannot give you an accurate equation to describe that love. Yet I can tell you how it feels and even why we love

19. *From the lecture* Is Art a Relationship or a Commodity? *presented to Interface Arts conference in Edinburgh, 2008.*

one another. I can write a poem to describe my love for her or even paint a picture. You might be able to relate to these expressions of love but they will be subject to the unique and personal experiences of your own relationships. They are subjective and non-accurate, but this is not to say that they are false. Far from it. Often, it is the artist who can help us understand the realities of love in a way that the sciences cannot.

... Ask questions

Some artwork will explore great and profound ideas such as the existential questions 'Why are we here?' and 'What is the purpose of life?' Other work will explore more modest themes such as 'Look at the fading flower'. Everything communicates something. Even the simplest drawing of a faded rose will communicate something of the artist's preferences and tastes, even the nature of beauty and decay.

We have already considered Paul's instruction to 'Test everything' (1 Thess 5:21) and Jesus' encouragement for us to have faith like little children (Matt 18:3). We might say that the artist is like a child, asking questions of the world until the world is either liberated or blue in the face with

frustration. We shouldn't be afraid to ask questions. In fact, we really must do so if we are to affirm that anything is true or real. Before Thomas could trust that Jesus really had risen from the dead he had first to doubt. Jesus wasn't angry at his questions but invited him to test his wounds to see if he was real.

... Tell stories

Jesus was a great storyteller. He used parables to describe the Kingdom of God in a way that expanded the imaginations of his hearers and was different from mere giving of facts and rhetoric. Art is a great vehicle for telling stories about Jesus, his creation and the new life to come.

Every story, whether Christian or not, is part of God's big story, the good story (or gospel) that Jesus Christ is Lord of everything. Some of us will tell profound stories that take on great and complex themes about life, the universe and everything. Others will tell a story that is as simple as 'Look at that fading flower'.[20] There is no story or subject that is outside the Lordship of Jesus Christ. The diversity in subject matter of our stories is rainbow rich. We needn't feel pressured to crow-bar a gospel message into each painting or

20. *I am indebted to artist Peter Smith who expanded on this idea in a lecture given at Interface Arts conference in Kent, 2009.*

song—through time, we can build a repertoire of stories that captivate the imaginations of our hearers with the truths of God. But the way in which we tell our stories requires a framework: every story needs a medium to be expressed in, and we need to think as hard about *how* we tell our stories as we do about getting the *content* of the message right.

… Remember and lament

Betty Spackman opens her book *A Profound Weakness* with the words, 'We make art to remind us of the invisible and to heal our forgetfulness.'[21]

In the Old Testament we read many times that the people erected memorial stones. For example, 'Samuel took a stone and set it up between Mizpah and Shen. He named it Ebenezer, saying, "Thus far has the Lord helped us"' (1 Sam 7:12). Art can help us remember important events of the past and what the Lord has done for us. It can also help us remember the more tragic events of our lives to help us mourn or lament.

There is much that we should lament in the fallen world. We see much lamentation in the books of Ecclesiastes, Job, Psalms and the prophets especially. Lamentation is an important biblical genre that is, perhaps, not particularly apparent in contemporary evangelical churches. The Christian mustn't shy away from subject matter that is difficult or painful. In many ways, it should be Christians who tell the most harrowing and despairing of stories because we know just how much God weeps over the sins of his people. We look forward to the return of Christ who will wipe away our tears, but he will also come as judge to punish and destroy. We must weep dearly for the suffering of this world and share the grief of those who are mourning.

Q: What do you think is the task of the artist today? Where do you agree and disagree with the list above? What other responsibilities would you include?

Q: What role can *your* art play in the arts today?

21. A Profound
    Weakness, *p. 3.*

Beyond Air Guitar

An interval

Not to us, O Lord, not to us
but to your name be the glory,
because of your love and faithfulness.

Psalm 115:1

Deep in the darkest recesses of my parents' garage, sandwiched between boxes of old records and videotapes, I recently came across a much-loved object from my childhood. To anyone else, it would have looked like any other old battered tennis racket but to me this was no ordinary Wilson Raleigh Junior. This meagre tennis racket had been my axe of power, my goblet of wrath, my chrome-plated Flying V with custom pick-ups and leopard-skin strap. This was my air guitar.

If you've ever fancied yourself as a bedroom rock-star you too might have spent nights in front of your parents' mirror raising an imaginary plectrum to the ceiling and strumming down with full rock fury as you played alone to your favourite bands. Of course, you may prefer the air drums or bass. My sister used to pretend her silver hairbrush was a microphone and sing along to Madonna. I caught myself doing it at a wedding reception recently to the tunes of Dire Straits, much to the embarrassment of everyone around me. They make 'air guitar' albums these days. You can go to the international air-guitar championships in America (how do they judge that?). It must be wrong. All so very wrong.

The trouble is, as vivid as our imaginations may be, air guitar will never feel the same or come anywhere close to actually being the real thing. It's all twang and no substance; escapist fantasy at its best. Beyond the ability to press the play button, air guitar requires absolutely no real skill, ability or talent. It may be brilliant entertainment but air guitar never really adds anything to the music or, for that matter, to creative culture. Sometimes, for us Christians in the creative arts, it can be a bit like we're playing the air guitar.

Beyond Air
Guitar

Sometimes we play air guitar to creative culture

In the book of Genesis, Adam and Eve were commissioned by God to bear fruit in all creation and to 'fill the earth and subdue it' (Gen 1:28). As we'll see in the following chapters, this creation mandate informed every area of life on the planet, including the creative arts. When God created the world it was very good. As those made in his image our mandate is to make culture of the highest standard. We are to pioneer and steward in the arts, leading by example, not following the crowd, and to set a generous example to the rest of the world.

Sometimes we are tempted to merely imitate what we see around us because it is easier for us or more comfortable: the Christian band whose lyrics may be biblically 'sound' but who sound just like everybody else in the charts, the Christian painter who prays for God to make his art great but who just doesn't put in the hours to really make it so, or the Christian designer who wants to produce quality but feels the pressure because there's too much other work to do. Jesus said that we Christians are the salt and light of the world. Our art should bring flavour, healing and illumination to those it reaches, but sometimes it's hard to do that when all we're thinking about are the bills to pay and mouths at home to feed. Making great art takes time, energy, graft, study and prayer. Before the fall work would have been a delight to Adam, but it has become hard. The creative soil of the arts is difficult to plough, taking the sweat off our brows. However, through the healing power of God's Spirit, the inspiration of his word, the encouragement of fellowship and the powerful tool of prayer, we do have great possibilities for making art that not only brings a blessing to the world today but may continue to bear cultural fruit for generations to come.

Sometimes we play air guitar to God

The apostle Paul wrote to the church in Colosse, 'Whatever you do, work at it with all your heart, as working for the Lord, not for men' (Col 3:23). We are instructed to be creative for Christ: to sing, dance, sculpt, design, model, write, compose and paint with all our hearts for the glory of God. The creative arts were created by God, belong to him and were designed to give him glory. Therefore, in every act of creativity we should work with all our hearts as working for the Lord and not for men. When we sing, our voices echo in the presence of the Ancient of Days. When we exhibit, our art is displayed before the King of kings. Our creativity is an act of living sacrifice to the Lord and should therefore demonstrate the best of our efforts, being aromatic and pleasing to his name.

As Christ described himself as 'the truth' we who follow him should make art that reflects his truth. Our art should be authentic. Authentic art is genuine and original, as opposed to fake or a reproduction. Authentic art moves beyond 'air guitar' mimicry—but this is not to say that Christians shouldn't imitate. Far from it; the apostle Paul suggested that Christians should imitate him (1 Cor 4:16) just as he imitated Christ. It is good to take inspiration from those who have gone before us and whose great art we aspire to emulate, but imitation should always be an act of tribute and not mere copying or plagiarism.

In the past the church has inspired and commissioned great works of art that have been a blessing to society for centuries and generations. Now it is our turn to make culture for Christ. Where are the artists of God today? Where are the designers, musicians, writers, sculptors and architects who consider everything as loss compared to the wonder of knowing Christ and making him known in the creative industries? Where are the artisans who would compromise nothing, working with all their hearts and with prayer to make art, through the redemptive power of God's Spirit, that is truly excellent for their Lord? As those made in the image of God we have a biblical mandate to be creative, to sing, paint, write, dance, cook, design, compose and perform for the glory of God. We make new modes of culture and explore new ways of seeing as those commissioned by God to work in the arts and fulfil something of our communal task to steward every aspect of his creation. We don't play along to culture, neither do we segregate from it or become partisan; but working within the creative industries that God created and first called 'good' we are as shrewd as snakes and as innocent as doves as we listen, speak and create for Christ.

Art and the Bible

Introduction

Epic in its scope, magnificent in its render and magnanimous in its message, the Bible is a majestic tour de force of creative writing and a glorious work of art in its own right.

The apostle Paul writes to Timothy, 'All Scripture is God-breathed [Greek *theopneustos*]' (2 Tim 3:16). When we read the Bible we are reading the revelation of the Creator God himself. The Bible is also crafted by the hands of individual writers and therefore reflects the unique styles, tastes and cultural influences of those who penned it. As a body of writing the Bible is truly remarkable and no other work of art has ever been produced in this way.

Today we pick up a copy of the Bible that is neatly bound with crisp white pages and nicely packaged in a choice of colours, shapes and sizes, but we should remember that the Bible, primarily, is a collection of 66 books of varying genres and styles, written over centuries and representative of diverse societies and cultures. The Bible presents us with an abundance of writing genres including poetry, rhetoric, law, sermons, prophecy, letters, lamentation, songs, monologues, dialogues and liturgy, to name just a few. Compare, for example, the lamentations of David's psalms—a songwriter whom Bono describes as 'the greatest blues writer of all time'[22]—with the apocalyptic imagery of Revelation written by the apostle John—whom playwright Blake Morrison describes as 'inspiring and sensuous, an enigmatic guide ... a poet through and through'.[23]

When we read God's word we are engaging with historical documents that tell us much about the people, art and cultural traditions of those who lived a very long time ago. Yet I am convinced that the Bible is the authoritative word of God, uniquely inspired by God's Spirit, and is therefore living, active and relevant to us now. It is 'useful for teaching, rebuking, correcting and training in righteousness' (2 Tim 3:16) just as much today as it was when first penned all those years ago.

In this section we will delve deep into the pages of the Bible to see the glory of the risen Christ. We will attempt to uncover God's intentions for the creative arts from the beginning, through the fall and redemption to the renewal of the creation. We will consider how to apply God's word to the arts today and look forward to the wonder of art in the great and glorious future new creation.

We will begin in the early chapters of Genesis with God's initial design for his world and people. Personally, I see the opening chapters as a theological account of the creation story and not a literal record of how God created the world (although many Christians have different views on this). I believe that Genesis describes the intelligent design of our universe by God with intention, order and purpose, using language that deliberately appeals to the imagination just as much as it stimulates our reasoning.

The Psalmist sang about God's word as being 'a lamp to my feet and a light for my path' (Ps 119:105), a shield, a fortress and 'sweeter than honey' (Ps 119 and 19:10). We don't often think of reading the Bible as a sensory experience but the Psalmist suggests that we should. When was the last time you let the words of the Bible drip off your lips like sweet-tasting honey?

22. *From his introduction to the Pocket Canon edition of the Book of Psalms (Canongate Books, 1996).*

23. *From his introduction to the Pocket Canon edition of John's Gospel (Canongate Books, 1996).*

The Bible gives examples of artists, such as Jubal, the father of all music (Gen 4:21), the psalmist David and good old Bezalel (Exod 31), who was commissioned directly by God to make art for the tabernacle and whom we will discuss in detail. We see evidence of creative evangelism in the prophecies of Hosea, Amos and Ezekiel, who performed a form of play in front of the gates to Jerusalem (Ezek 4), and not least in the parables of Jesus, who could hold the attention of an audience for hours on end.

It is rare to hear a sermon on the creative arts today yet the Bible is wonderfully rich in instruction for those who make art. I often wonder if biblical guidance on the arts is one of the best-kept secrets of the church today! So it's to this majestic, authoritative, creative, living, breathing word of God that we now turn for instruction but also for inspiration as we seek to serve Christ and make him known in the creative arts today.

8. In the Beginning

The creativity of God

Nature is too thin a screen; the glory of the omnipresent God bursts through everywhere.

Ralph Waldo Emerson, American poet and lecturer, 1803–1882[24]

O Lord, our Lord,
how majestic is your name in all the earth!
You have set your glory above the heavens.

Psalm 8

You only need to take a peek out the window on a plane, smell the freshly cut grass in the summer or listen to the birdsong in the forest to know that when God created the earth he made it really well. Even the skies recognize the greatness of their creator: 'The heavens declare the glory of God, the skies proclaim the work of his hands' (Ps 19:1). The creation can't keep quiet about how great God's creativity was: 'Day after day they pour forth speech; night after night they display knowledge' (v. 2).

Whilst the creation is fallen and frustrated we can look beyond the shadows to the glory of God's original design—the grandeur of the mountains, the spectacular colours of tropical fish, the beauty of the setting sun and the freshness of the morning dew—and we sing, 'How Great Thou art! How Great Thou art!' When God created, he created really well.

God is an excellent creator and the creativity of the Father was demonstrated in his Son, Jesus. Think about the time when Christ turned water into wine at the wedding in Cana. He didn't knock up any old brew, but he created the finest wine the guests had ever tasted. Jesus was also a master storyteller, holding the attention of his audience for hours on end and sometimes through the baking heat of the midday sun. When Jesus created, he created really well.

Since we are made in the image of God our art should reflect something of his excellent creativity. We are not called to perfection but, as we have seen, we are to strive hard in our art and work with all our hearts (Col 3:23).

In this chapter we'll think about how God created the world and look to his example as the author of all creativity for putting together a framework for our own art-making.

Q: Read through Genesis 1 and imagine that God is in a crit. How does God create? What is his design method and style?

24. *Quoted from www.thinkexist. com.*

> In the beginning God created …
> (Gen 1:1)

Isn't it reassuring to know that the very first thing God chose to record about his own character in his word, the Bible, was his own creativity? We know that God is for the creative arts. He invented them and is Lord over them. God isn't just a creator; he is *the* Creator with a capital 'C'!

In the beginning …

… There was anticipation

> In the beginning God created the heavens and the earth. Now the earth was formless and empty, darkness was over the surface of the deep, and the Spirit of God was hovering over the waters.
> (Gen 1:1,2)

Before God created, the earth was formless and empty. It would be a mistake to assume that there was chaos before the creation because God's sovereign rule was present and manifest through his Spirit hovering over the waters.

The Spirit of God (or breath—*ruach*— of God) hovered over the waters, perhaps resembling a great composer in the moments before the baton

falls or the painter in that moment of anticipation before the first strike of the canvas. God breathed—a moment's pause—and then creation! By the power of his Word God brought forth form, content, structure, order, arrangement, shape, pattern, composition, light and an explosion of life from the depths of the darkness.

… There was authentic creation

> And God said, 'Let there be light', and there was light. God saw that the light was good, and he separated the light from the darkness. God called the light 'day', and the darkness he called 'night'. And there was evening, and there was morning—the first day.
> (Gen 1:3–5)

When God created he had only to speak and matter came into being. God, and only God, can make something from nothing. I've been painting for over 25 years but I'm not yet able to say, 'Let there be art!' and have a brilliant painting materialize in front of my eyes. We could say that God is therefore the only 'true' or 'authentic' creator. In contrast, we are re-creators who make from the materials God has first created. As a painter I can only paint because God has first created colour, lines, paint and the landscape. A musician can only compose because God has first given us melody, harmony, rhythm and the heartbeat.

… There was autonomous creation

It doesn't appear as though God suffered from writer's block. From day one there was an explosion of creation filling the whole earth. Where did his ideas come from? As we know that God, and only God, existed before the creation we can conclude that God's creation was born out of his own character. In contrast, we source ideas from the world around us. We read in Ecclesiastes, 'there is nothing new under the sun' (Eccl 1:9); we are limited to finding inspiration for our work from what has already been seen although we may make something new or reinvent. God, on the other hand, demonstrated his capacity for uniquely autonomous creation.

… Creativity was relational

Before there was creation there was relationship. Before God created

the world a relationship existed between the three figureheads of the Trinity. God the Father was there at the beginning and the Spirit of God was also hovering over the waters. In John 1 we also read that Jesus was there at the beginning, the *logos* (or Word) of God. The apostle Paul wrote, 'all things were created *by* him [Christ] and *for* him' (Col 1:16, emphasis added). The universe was created through the creative relationship among the Trinity.

This is important to note as it illustrates the making of art as a primarily relational activity. Art is not just a commodity to be bought and sold, nor is it a mere expression of the self; it is a form of communication between the artist and his or her audience.

… There was critique

> God saw that the light was good.
> (Gen 1:4)

There are two things to note here. First, God's creative method included a form of self-evaluation. Second, God said that his work was 'good' six times in Genesis 1 and concluded that altogether, it was 'very good'. Imagine you have just finished a piece of work and a friend or tutor asks you if you are happy with it and you say, 'It is good … Actually, it is *very* good!' If we were to say what God said of his creation we might come across as arrogant or vain, but God is not egotistic: the creation really was that good. He was declaring a statement of fact as well as of praise.

What then can we draw from this moment of evaluation in the creation story? At first, the right response would be to agree with God in praising him for his creation! We join with all creation in singing the praises of the Creator God! We could also say that God's example demonstrates for us the freedom to evaluate our own work, but we need to do this with truthfulness, integrity and with the help of others who know what they are on about. If the work is good we should be free to say, 'It is good.' No false modesty here! If the work needs improvement we should have the humility to go back to working on it or to learn from our mistakes and move on. As all art is fallen (because all the creation is fallen) it is unlikely that a painting will be either *all* good or *all* bad. Something might be identified as positive whilst other aspects need to be rejected or worked out better. Art criticism was not a human invention but was demonstrated by the character of God.

… There was order, structure and harmony

> … and he separated the light from the darkness. (Gen 1:4)

As the creation story unfolds we see God developing the forms he created through separating the light from darkness, sky from water and land from sea. Creation is made more complex through division. On day three God returns to what he made on day one by forming a sun and stars to govern the day and the night. On day five he returns to the sky and waters created by division on day two and populates them with birds and fish. Finally on day six he returns to the land and sea created on day three and enriches his design through the creation of animals and man, the crowning glory of the creation.

This makes sense of our own creative process. If we are painters, we begin with the elementary colours and divide them to form new and more complex colours. We return to work we have made on a previous day and show invention as we work into the shapes, tones and composition already established to make it more complex, nuanced and aesthetically rich.

In the creation there was a symmetry that exhibited God's intention and order in the creative process. Today, this means that it makes sense for us to be intentional in our art as we plan our use of time, money and other resources. There is a 'natural rhythm' to God's creativity. In our own creative practices it is good to reflect something of God's sense of order and structure. Just as God explored new ideas within a theme so it is good for us to push ideas until they are mature, complete or exposed as useless.

Art can reflect the creativity of God through bringing order and shape to empty forms. We may not have the stars and planets at our disposal but we can bring structure and meaning to the materials we have to hand. A musician can create meaning by crafting notes and melodies to make new sounds. A writer can make meaning from words and sentences. A sculptor takes the formless entity of shapeless clay and makes something new and wonderful that has never been seen before. In all of these ways we reflect the creativity of the God who brought order, meaning, rhythm and life from the formless void of the empty darkness.

… God named his creation

> God called the light 'day', and the darkness he called 'night'. (Gen 1:5)
>
> God called the expanse 'sky'. (Gen 1:8)
>
> God called the dry ground 'land', and the gathered waters he called 'seas'. (Gen 1:10)

Do you see how at the end of every day God named what he had created that day? It's as if naming his work was the final thing to do before packing it in for the night. Naming is an important part of any creative process. Think about what names achieve and how they function in the creative process. A name will categorize one item and distinguish it from another, such as 'land' from 'sea'. Names give context to an object; they provide it with an identity and status within the world.

When you were born your parents gave you a name as a sign of identity but also as a mark of their authority over your life. As a child you belonged to them. In the same way God illustrated his ownership of creation by naming it.

It's the privilege of an author to name their book, just as a songwriter has the right to title their song. Even if the title is 'Untitled' it still gives a context to the work in which the art can be read.

God placed great value upon names. Think of all the Old Testament characters whose names described their characters, such as Jacob, 'the deceiver', and his unfortunately named older brother, Esau, which means 'red and hairy'. Today we pray in the name of the Lord Jesus, which means that we are praying according to his will. Since names are of great value to God I suggest it is important that we consider our titles well when it comes to our own work.

… God took a break

> And there was evening, and there was morning—the first day. (Gen 1:5)

As a student I was often reminded by my tutors of the great legacy of artists who had studied at the Glasgow School of Art. We stood on the shoulders of great giants: an experience that singularly inspired and intimidated me at the same time. One tutor used to tell us about a student called Jenny Saville who

went on to achieve great things in the contemporary painting world. Keen to learn something from her success we asked our tutor what she was like as a student. To our surprise, he said she was hardly ever in the studio! She had spent as much time away from the easel, taking breaks at the local cinema and going for walks around the park, as she did in front of it. The point is that her breaks were part of her creating process: valuable times of refreshment for gathering her thoughts before coming back in to work. I wish my breaks were so productive.

Taking a break is an important part of the creative process. If you write, paint or perform you may find that your better moments of inspiration come at the most inconvenient times: when you're in the shower or driving your car. As we read the creation story it is striking how God paused at the end of every day. There was a purposeful break in activity between the evening and the morning of every day.

God didn't work flat out then crash on the seventh day; the creation pattern had a rhythm of production that we can learn from. It's important during the working day to take a break, to enjoy a cup of tea or to chat with a studio mate. This can be a very godly thing to do. Sometimes the most productive thing to do is to go home at the end of the day and get a good night's sleep then come in the next day with fresh eyes to see the work again. Whilst God never slept or popped back to his flat for the night that's certainly the *model* he gives us, and if that's how God works why should we try to be any different?

… There was rest

> By the seventh day God had finished the work he had been doing; so on the seventh day he rested from all his work. And God blessed the seventh day and made it holy, because on it he rested from all the work of creating that he had done. (Gen 2:2,3)

Taking a break is different from having a good long rest. At the end of the creation story God stopped creating and rested. This was something more than a night off or a tea break; this was a long opportunity to step back from the work, admire it and evaluate what he had done. It wasn't as if God was exhausted by the work, as 'he who watches over Israel will neither slumber nor sleep' (Ps 121:4), yet God models a Sabbath day to us for rest and reflection.

To the Israelites the Sabbath day wasn't just about catching up with sleep, it was also a day for rejoicing and remembering what God had done for them in bringing them out of slavery in Egypt. Just as the Israelites were commanded to keep the Sabbath day holy, so Christians continue to meet once a week for communal worship of God and 'family time' with the church. The Sabbath is a day of community and it is helpful for us artists to be with others who are different from us and to hear God's word preached. We all know what happens when we don't rest: burnout sets in and the work suffers.

God's creation proclaims the greatness of his character through the wonder of his works. We see an intelligent designer who created with imagination and order. I am amazed that the outline of a sprawling river delta can also be reflected in the pattern of a leaf, revealing God's concern for both the great and the minute within his creation. To me, God's attention to detail is as breathtaking as the scale of his project. This is the God we worship and whose image we bear.

Not that perfection is required of us, but the model for creativity does demand much indeed. It is my prayer that as a generation of Christian artists we will aim high in the standard of our art to make excellent work for our Lord, bringing glory to the Creator.

Q: What else do you see in the model for creativity God gave us in the beginning?

Q: How can you reflect the character of God in your own creative processes and practices?

9. Arte Factum

Making art in the image of God

Art making has value to God because making art is a form of creativity. Creativity is valuable because it is part of God's character and as humans we have been made in God's image as creative beings.

Francis Schaeffer, *Art and the Bible*[25]

Well I heard there was a secret chord that David played and it pleased the Lord.

Leonard Cohen, songwriter

What does it mean to be human? As Christians, we believe that our purpose and identity in creation are ontologically connected to the likeness we bear to our Creator God. But what does this mean in practice?

> God created man
> in his own image,
> in the image of God
> he created him;
> male and female
> he created them. (Gen 1:27)

To create is to be human

As those made in God's image, we inherit many of his attributes. God is a spiritual being, so we have a spirit; God is a physical being,[26] so we have physicality; God is moral,

relational and social, so we have the ability to make decisions about right and wrong, we look for relationships to find fulfilment and we are part of communities such as families, friendships, peer groups, churches and societies. All these attributes of our humanity originate in God's character.

To be creative is simply part of what it means to be human, so we don't have to justify our art by writing Bible verses in the bottom right-hand corner or trying to crow-bar a gospel message into a design for a chair. The making of art is as human an action as eating a meal, going to sleep or enjoying a conversation.

Q: If being creative is part of what it means to be human do all acts of creativity bring glory to God?

Q: How do we know when we are creating in a way that pleases the Lord? When do we know if we are not?

It's not as simple as saying that God likes paintings of churches but hates pictures of blood, guts and gore. Nor can we say all Christians make 'good' art inherently because of their belief in God. A work of art can be excellently rendered but

25. Nottingham: IVP, 2009.

26. In that he manifests himself through the Creation and becomes incarnate in physical form as Jesus Christ.

demonstrate a godless worldview. In the same way Christians can make art that has a good message but is rendered without consideration.

The Bible gives various accounts of art that either pleased the Lord or brought him grief. In the next chapter we'll look at what the Bible says about idols and the kind of art that God hates, but for now let's sit under the tutorship of some of the great biblical artists who rendered art that gave great glory to God. The cultural landscape for the arts has changed since biblical times and the function of art in society is different today, but from their examples we can still draw principles for our own creative ventures.

Art-man Adam: the first artist in the Bible

When it comes to biblical examples of art that pleased the Lord we really are spoilt for choice. The very first person to 'make with skill' (*arte factum*) in the Bible was Adam: 'The Lord God took the man and put him in the Garden of Eden to work it and take care of it' (Gen 2:15). On his first day of existence, Adam was set to work in the Garden of Eden, stewarding the land and taking care of what God had created. This very creative and important task involved more than watering the plants: Adam was responsible for the social, ecological and administrative order of everything God had given to him. This privilege began with a specific duty, a creative responsibility that, until now, had been performed only by God himself: he was to name the animals:

MADE IN THE FATHER'S IMAGE

Now the Lord God had formed out of the ground all the beasts of the field and all the birds of the air. He brought them to the man to see what he would name them; and whatever the man called each living creature, that was its name. So the man gave names to all the livestock, the birds of the air and all the beasts of the field. (Gen 2:19–20)

We already know the significance of naming creation from our study in Genesis 1. What an enormous privilege for Adam to join in the creative process in this way! If naming the creation was part of the creative act itself, here God was trusting Adam with a delegation of global significance.

This would have been quite a long day for Adam. Imagine being faced with the flamingo or armadillo. What would you have called them? In delegating the naming of the animals to Adam, God consolidated mankind's status as custodians of the creation. Just as God is Lord over all creation so man, in his image, was made warden over the creation.

The creation order still stands today as God never retracted his commission for mankind to work

in his creation and take care of it. In the creative arts, as in every area of the world, we are still to show dominion and stewardship: initiative and responsibility.

Adam's love song

When Adam named the animals he was responding to God's instruction to be creative, but his second act of creativity came completely unprompted, simply as an expression of his humanity.

Not everything in creation was good. In Genesis 2:18 we read, 'It is not good for the man to be alone.' This seems to have been one of the reasons why Adam was instructed to name the animals; we are later told that 'for Adam no suitable helper was found' among the animal kingdom (the wildebeest was not an appropriate wife for Adam. Go figure). God therefore caused Adam to fall into a deep sleep, removed a rib from his side and set to work sculpting his ideal partner: 'Then the Lord God made a woman from the rib he had taken out of the man, and he brought her to the man' (Gen 2:22).

Can you imagine Adam's state of mind on first encountering his wife,

Eve? He's never seen a woman before and one morning, when he wakes, perhaps wiping the sleep from his eyes, he finds this vision of beauty resting beside him: his perfect partner, his wife and lover ... and she is naked. If you are married or have been in love you might relate to Adam's feelings as he fell in love for the first time. As for many of us, love inspired him to write poetry.

> The man said,
> 'This is now bone of my bones
> and flesh of my flesh;
> she shall be called "woman"
> for she was taken out of man.'
> (Gen 2:23)

Adam wrote poetry for Eve. It might not quite compare to Shakespeare's poetry but it functions perfectly well as a little poem. There's even a little wordplay: the name 'woman' (Hebrew *ishshah*) derives from the name 'man' (Hebrew *iysh*), just as Eve had come from the side of Adam. Note that God didn't instruct Adam to be creative; Adam was writing poetry because he was a human being. This was a poem about identity, status and ownership. Today it might not sound very politically correct but here, before the fall, Adam was articulating something of the relationship he and his new wife would share. Note

that this was not a hymn about God or his attributes, yet God was present and therefore, we assume, supportive of Adam's creative efforts.

Adam's creativity was the blueprint for human enjoyment of creativity without fear of reproach or condemnation from God. We can paint, sculpt, write, sing and make all kinds of art simply as a gift of grace and for the pleasure and enjoyment of God's good creation.

Adam was not a 'professional' artist but there are others in the Old Testament to whom we may be able to relate more keenly as they were employed to make art.

Crafty-boy Bezalel: the first professional artist

Perhaps the most descriptive account of professional art-making in the Bible concerns the art of the tabernacle, completed by Bezalel and his collective of designers and craftsmen in Exodus 31. To give a little context, we jump into this story as the Israelites are in exile, freed from the slavery of Egypt but still in the desert on their way to the promised land, a land 'flowing with milk and honey' (Exod 3:8,17).

In itself the exodus is a great picture of the gospel as the people were delivered from oppression and were now free. Like us, they lived in exile like aliens in the world, looking forward to the fulfilment of their inheritance and the realization of the promised future kingdom. God instructed them to build a tabernacle at the centre of their camp to signify God's presence in their midst. The tabernacle was the dwelling of God's heavenly presence on earth and right at the heart of his people, and it was crammed full of art. God wanted his own house to be adorned with beautiful art.

> Then the Lord said to Moses, 'See, I have chosen Bezalel son of Uri, the son of Hur, of the tribe of Judah, and I have filled him with the Spirit of God, with skill, ability and knowledge in all kinds of crafts—to make artistic designs for work in gold, silver and bronze, to cut and set stones, to work in wood, and to engage in all kinds of craftsmanship.' (Exod 31:1–5)

The hero of our story is Bezalel. Not one of the most notorious characters of the Old Testament, and you probably wouldn't name your kid after him, but Bezalel is important,

not only because God thought him worthy to appear in his eternal word, the Bible, but also because Bezalel is the first person in the Bible who we are told was filled with the Spirit of God for a specific task. And that task was to make art.

This is something I love about Bezalel's story. Not that we should read too much into it, but isn't it interesting that the first person mentioned in the Bible as being specifically filled with God's Spirit is not a warrior, king or prophet, but a lesser-known artist?

'The Ark' (after Bezalel – after God's design)

We're told that Bezalel was chosen out of all the people of Israel to be filled with 'skill, ability and knowledge in all kinds of crafts'. Bezalel would have worked hard at his art. There is no indication that his gift simply fell from the sky one day or downloaded straight into his brain. It's quite possible he was an apprentice at one point and the level of his ability models to us the importance of hard graft.

Getting the right materials

> ... make artistic designs for work in gold, silver and bronze, to cut and set stones, to work in wood, and to engage in all kinds of craftsmanship. (Exod 31:4,5)

Interestingly, the materials used to build the tabernacle were very expensive. God wanted good materials for his house and chose the raw materials of stone, bronze, silver and gold. As the story is repeated in chapter 35 we read about precious jewels, fine linen, acacia wood and expensive purple dyes. This wasn't about a quick dash to B&Q for a tub of emulsion; only the best was good enough for the Lord.

All the art materials came from the people, being donated freely by the Israelite community who, we must presume, saw value in giving fine materials for God's purposes. Later, in chapter 36 we read how the Israelites gave so many precious things that Moses had to tell them to stop! As Christians we are free to use a diversity of materials and artists shouldn't feel restricted or guilty for choosing fine materials (unless, of course, they put them in debt). It is not holy to use cheaper materials just because it saves money. The materials we use should be the right materials for the job—nothing more, nothing less; yet it is important to note that God's people used the finest materials for the purposes of worship.

Collaboration, unity and ...

When I was a teenager I used to play in a garage band with a couple of mates. We achieved a certain degree of local fame but I don't think you could ever say we were going to give U2 a run for their money! The greatest thrill in playing with the band was knocking out new ideas together in the studio: jamming out new material on our lead guitarist's porch, which terrified the neighbouring cows as he lived on a farm. As a band, we shared everything together: ideas, dreams and even money, as we worked towards our common goal of making the best kind of music we possibly could.

Since we are made in God's image we are designed to work together in community, reflecting the communal actions of the Trinity. We see this demonstrated in Adam, who was not designed to be on his own but to have a partner in Eve. We see it in the manner in which God called his chosen people Israel to live as a nation centred around the tabernacle. We also see it in the way God commissioned the art of the tabernacle itself, as Bezalel worked in collaboration with others such as Oholiab (another name you probably won't be giving to one of your children) and the group of artists he instructed and mentored (Exod 35:34).

Sometimes it can be hard work, as egos conflict and ideas clash, but working in collaboration is one of the most enriching principles the Bible encourages us as artists to adopt. Collaboration can bring great blessing. It provides support and a framework for advice and professional criticism. Those who collaborate can share one another's successes as well as their failures. They can hold one another accountable and encourage excellence and the pursuit of godly ambitions, whilst also challenging and rebuking one another when motivations have become sinful.

27. Bearing Fresh Olive Leaves *(Carlisle: Piquant, 2000), p. 43.*

Calvin Seerveld was on to a good thing when he wrote,

> Christian artists, scattered like sheep in a thousand studios, schools and offices, belong together professionally in trying to be faithful in having the Lord's kingdom come on earth as it is in heaven. They should recognize that truth openly by organising themselves as part of the body of Christ bound together by a common, biblical Christian confession. With members at different stages of having their personal and professional lives brought into line with their Holy Spirit filled hearts, they are able to build one another up in artistry, not just in prayer breakfasts and fellowship meetings but also in actual, professional Christian art edification.[27]

... Diversity

The tabernacle would have provided worshippers with an extravagant multisensory experience, with its diversity of design that reflected the nature of God's creation itself: 'He has filled them with skill to do all kinds of work as craftsmen, designers, embroiderers in blue, purple and scarlet yarn and fine linen, and weavers—all of them master craftsmen and designers' (Exod 35:35).

In Exodus 32–35 we see a broad spectrum of art represented in the tabernacle, including tapestry, sculpture, wall sculpture, jewellery, lamp-stands, tables, incense burners and textiles. Exodus 30 gives detailed instructions for the incense. There was two-dimensional art, three-dimensional sculpture, music, ceremony and even clothing design: Exodus 28 speaks of the designer garments worn by the priests in the most holy part of the Tabernacle, giving specific detail for everything right down to the cleanliness of the priests' underwear and the collar-line of Aaron's tunic: 'Make the robe of the ephod entirely of blue cloth, with an opening for the head in its centre. There shall be a woven edge like a collar around this opening, so that it will not tear' (Exod 28:31,32).

Why did God want so much art in his house? We could speculate that it was simply because he is a great lover of diverse art. God was as interested in the form as he was in the function of articles designed for communal worship. The sheer diversity of the creative arts represented at this one pivotal point in the history of God's people provides, I believe, great liberation for all who want to serve God through their art. We are free to sculpt, sing, write, perform, design and compose in any discipline we choose.

Working professionally in the arts

Whilst there is much we can learn from the examples of Adam and Bezalel they are limited in their application for the creative industries today, as Adam created for pleasure and Bezalel worked to a specific design brief in the context of communal worship. Many of us take pleasure from working professionally in the arts but we also have very real concerns, such as paying the bills and working to a client's brief. In the same way, whilst some make art within the context of church institutions, many of us are employed in the wider field of the creative arts, outside church walls. There are, however, many principles we can apply to our work from the examples of Adam and Bezalel. Creativity is both a gift and a mandate to the church for the world, whether we make art as a hobby or for a living.

Q: What can you learn from Adam's and Bezalel's examples for your own creative practice?

Q: How were Adam's and Bezalel's situations different from your experience of the arts today? Where are there similarities?

Q: What needs to happen next in the studio? How will you apply what you have read in Genesis and Exodus in your current work?

10. My Idol

Art after the fall

If I had said television is more popular than Jesus, I might have got away with it.

John Lennon, dead musician[28]

Q: What is an idol and how do you know when you're worshipping one?

Q: What are you most tempted to idolize in the arts world?

My favourite idol growing up was Kurt Cobain

When I was growing up my idol was Kurt Cobain. I wore my jeans like Kurt, wore my hair like his and had a T-shirt exactly like the one he always used to wear. There wasn't much to do in my home town except play football and start bands so, since I was embarrassingly bad at the former, I found myself getting into the latter in a big way (the football lads were all into bands like D:Ream, Oasis and Right Said Fred anyway). Most weekends I'd go round to my mate John's house and we'd listen to The Wonder Stuff, Pulp, Blur, Oasis, The Stone Roses, Counting Crows, Nirvana. Stuff like that.

We didn't just want to look like Kurt Cobain; we or Cobain. We wanted to *be* Kurt Cobain, dressing exactly the same way as him with our ripped jeans, Converse trainers and grunge T-shirts. Some of my mates even bleached their hair but I never had the guts to be that rebellious; my mum would have killed me if I'd done anything like that. We formed bands to prove that we were different from everybody else. We wrote songs to stand out from the crowd.

We all have idols in our lives. For some of us it's flesh-and-blood idols, like rock stars and artists. For others it's money, careers, sex, status, houses and things like that. But whether our idols are real or imagined, personified or idealistic, God's word is clear: all idols are a poor substitute for the one true God and need to be rooted out of our lives.

28. John Lennon as interviewed at a news conference in Chicago 11 August 1966. Reference thanks to http://beatlesnumber9.com/biggerjesus.html

Stealing worship

Let's get one thing straight. When it comes to worship there's only one hero who deserves our full adoration. If you want to be like someone, be like Jesus Christ. Compared with worshipping him, all other forms of worship are just plain foolish. This is how the apostle Paul put it to the Romans: 'Although they claimed to be wise, they became fools and exchanged the glory of the immortal God for images made to look like mortal man and birds and animals and reptiles' (Rom 1:22,23). Can you hear the frustration in Paul's voice? How stupid can we really be? Although we claim to be intelligent, rational beings we still think that having our faces on the front covers of magazines will make us happy; we still want trophies for our mantelpieces; and we still dream of being on *Top of the Pops*.

The Psalmist warns that idols consume the human heart. He describes how, through time, we become like the very things we idolize.

> Not to us, O Lord, not to us
> but to your name be the glory,
> because of your love
> and faithfulness.
> Why do the nations say,
> 'Where is their God?'
> Our God is in heaven;
> he does whatever pleases him.
> But their idols are silver and gold,
> made by the hands of men.
> They have mouths, but cannot speak,
> eyes, but they cannot see;
> they have ears, but cannot hear,
> noses, but they cannot smell;
> they have hands, but cannot feel,
> feet, but they cannot walk;
> nor can they utter a sound with their throats.
> Those who make them will be like them,
> and so will all who trust in them. (Ps 115:1–8)

'Not to us, O Lord, not to us ...'

If there's one thing that will stand out in the creative arts and media it's genuine humility. Often the greatest idols in our own lives are ourselves. In an industry that encourages self-promotion and 'self-belief', how can we look for opportunities without selling out on humility? The Bible instructs us to 'Do nothing out of selfish ambition or vain conceit, but in humility consider others better than yourselves' (Phil 2:3).

Humility and self-deprecation are not the same thing. It's one thing to give a reasonable critique of your work but another to pretend there is nothing of worth there at all. When God made the world he saw that it was good and said so. If there is good in your work you must be able to recognize that and give thanks to your Father in heaven for gifting you with the ability to make art. Most artworks are neither absolutely 'good' nor absolutely 'bad' but can reflect varied values and weaknesses. If your work is weak in one area it's good to recognize that honestly and then try to improve—but also see the good.

'Those who make them will be like them ...'

I think this is a sobering statement for those of us who aspire to be something in the arts. But what does the Psalmist mean when he says that those who make idols 'will be like them'? Idols come with a whole world of baggage, having values and goals of their own. If you idolize the thought of becoming a rock star, for example, you will come to value what rock stars value; if you want to be like a certain artist you will be influenced by that artist's thinking and work. If your idol likes to throw TVs out of hotel windows, you're likely to have

some trouble with your parents when it comes to spring cleaning.

The things or people we aspire to be can often consume us as we take on their values and become like them. We might not look the same on the outside, but inside our hearts will be devoted to the pursuit of goals other than those God has prepared for us.

Sex and drugs and sausage rolls: how do you spot an idol?

Before the fall there were no idols as sin had not yet corrupted the affections of human hearts. After the fall, God's people built sculptures to bow down to in the place of God, such as the golden calf (Exod 32) and the bronze snake (2 Kings 18:4), which was made by God's command but later abused as an idol. People 'exchanged the glory of the immortal God for images made to look like mortal man and birds and animals and reptiles' (Rom 1:23). While in the beginning human creativity had given glory to God, now, after the fall, it was being used to steal worship away from him.

How do you know an idol when you see one? In Paul's day, it was quite easy to spot the idols in society. As he walked around Athens (see Acts 17) they were pretty easily identifiable as the statues on every street corner: the ones that represented what every Greek wanted to look like! The same could be said about the ancient Israelites. 'Where's the idol? That would be that big sculpture of a golden calf you're all dancing around and bowing down to.' In the absence of Moses, Aaron had given in to the people's wishes and fashioned a statue that became a form of substitute leader and God for them.

Even though we might not bow down to lumps of metal and carved stone today, that is not to say that we don't worship idols in other forms. Idols are symbols, pictures or ideas that embody something of what we want or crave in our lives. When we worship fame, success, celebrity or other vanities we are as guilty of idolatry today as the Athenians and Israelites were all those years ago. Whilst our idols might take different forms in the contemporary creative arts, they still rob our affections from God and entice us to worship the things of creation rather than the Creator himself.

There are some idols that we as artists find particularly enticing. Without wanting to over-generalize or stereotype—I am aware that my struggles will be different from

yours—I think that the following two are particular temptations for us artists: they are the idols of success and self.

Gimme, gimme, gimme: the idol of success

Many of us struggle, at some point, with the fear of anonymity. *What if no one recognizes me? What if no one sees my work?*

Whether it's the bad review, polite applause, a failed exam, a gallery rejection or the bad crit, we've all experienced some kind of rejection in the arts. This is a normal experience for all artists at some stage in their careers. We might catch ourselves asking why nobody 'gets' our work, or why they can't see how talented we really are.

At times, we may need to count our losses and retreat; recognizing when you've lost can be one of the signs of a healthy Christian who is secure in their identity in Christ. Thankfully God doesn't recognize success in the way the world does. Time and again through Scripture it is those who are ignored or written off by the world who go on to do the greatest things for God. Think of King David, who started off life as a shepherd boy and the youngest son in his family; or Gideon, who was so terrified of the Midianites that he hid in a wine-press; or Jonah, who was the biggest scaredy-cat of them all—yet God summoned a fish to swallow him and bring him back on track.

> But God chose the foolish things of the world to shame the wise; God chose the weak things of the world to shame the strong.' (1 Cor 1:27)

The Bible doesn't define success as the world does. Whilst we have an immediate audience of critics we have a primary audience of one who is more interested in our obedience and faithfulness to him than he is in how many awards we have won or how many friends we have on Facebook.

Me-me monster: the idol of self

'Look at me, look at me!' Since so much of what we do revolves around promoting our own art and the way we see the world, it's hard not to fall into the trap of selfish ambition and egotism. How often are we told to 'look after number one' and 'express yourself' because, as one cosmetics advert has it, 'you're worth it'?

In the Greek myth, Narcissus was so obsessed with himself that he died of starvation and thirst from just sitting by the edge of a pool until he gave out, gazing at his reflection until he died.

As Socrates famously said at his trial for heresy and corruption of the youth, 'The unexamined life is not worth living.' A good level of self-evaluation is necessary for a realistic grasp of how we're doing, but it's good to do this with others whom God has given to us to challenge us and encourage us. Let's avoid becoming like Narcissus, who obsessed over his image so much that he lost track of reality and brought about his own destruction.

How to smash an idol

There's no one-size-fits-all approach to fighting the idols in our lives but there are some helpful biblical principles we can follow.

Know your enemy

> Do not conform any longer to the pattern of this world, but be transformed by the renewing of your mind. Then you will be able to test and

approve what God's will is—his good, pleasing and perfect will. (Rom 12:2)

The first step to rooting out idols in our lives is to identify where they exist. This is where mates come in. It's often those closest to us who can see the things that are taking up too much of our time and attention. Ask your friends and family, 'Honestly, from the way I live my life, what do you think are the things that are most important to me?'

The best way to identify an idol is to hold it up to Jesus and compare them. Idols just look pathetic when they sit next to the magnificence and majesty of the risen Christ.

See the glory of Jesus

What is more, I consider everything a loss compared to the surpassing greatness of knowing Christ Jesus my Lord, for whose sake I have lost all things. (Phil 3:8)

God's word is clear by example and instruction that those who follow the one true God should do all they can to root out the idols that covet our devotion. The thing about idols

is that they pretend life would be better for us if we worshipped them, but there is nothing life-giving about an idol (a lump of stone does not have the ability to produce life). New life in Christ is so much better than a life enslaved to idols. Paul puts it like this:

Put to death, therefore, whatever belongs to your earthly nature: sexual immorality, impurity, lust, evil desires and greed, which is idolatry. Because of these, the wrath of God is coming. You used to walk in these ways, in the life you once lived. But now you must rid yourselves of all such things as these: anger, rage, malice, slander, and filthy language from your lips. Do not lie to each other, since you have taken off your old self with its practices and have put on the new self, which is being renewed in knowledge in the image of its Creator. (Col 3:5–10)

In the shop at the National Gallery in London there's a print of one of Monet's paintings of water lilies. It's not a bad reproduction but it's not a patch on the real thing that hangs two doors down in the gallery itself. Imagine going all the way to the gallery just to admire a reproduction in the shop when the beauty of the real thing is hanging right next door.

Jesus promised life in all its fulness (John 10:10). Worshipping anything other than the source of full life will lead only to disappointment and worse. Imagine living your life by a reproduction of the real God when we can know him, the one 'who is able to do immeasurably more than all we ask or imagine' (Eph 3:20).

Trust in the Saviour

> It is for freedom that Christ has set us free. Stand firm, then, and do not let yourselves be burdened again by a yoke of slavery. (Gal 5:1)

Jesus promised a new life for his followers, one no longer subject to the false traps of idols. If we take his words seriously we have to believe that it is possible to break our addictions to idols through the power of God. For many of us this will be a life-long struggle and we shouldn't expect an immediate change but 'the Lord is the Spirit, and where the Spirit of the Lord is, there is freedom' (2 Cor 3:17).

Change takes place in our lives when we turn to see the glory of Jesus. When we hear the gospel of Christ we see the glory of Christ with unveiled faces (2 Cor 4:4–6). When we come to Christ we are justified (made right) before God: our sins no longer stand against us. We are also sanctified (made holy) by the Spirit and this is an ongoing process as we say no to sin and choose to allow God's Spirit to be active in our lives.

Pray for change

> This is the confidence we have in approaching God: that if we ask anything according to his will, he hears us. And if we know that he hears us—whatever we ask—we know that we have what we asked of him. (1 John 5:14,15)

Since we know it is God's will for his children to be sanctified (1 Thess 4:3) we know that we are praying according to his will when we ask for help in rooting out the idols in our lives. If we have a God who loves us and is pleased to receive our exclusive affections we can know with confidence that he listens to our prayers and will help us.

My favourite worst idol and a prayer

When we were growing up we all had our own favourite idols. You now know that mine was Kurt Cobain. Today we may have new idols, such as success, power, celebrity, winning the Turner Prize, winning a BAFTA, money, status, fame—and the list goes on and on and on. Mostly, these idols are simply manifestations of our greatest idol, which is ourselves: our favourite worst idol. We know that anything that sets itself up against the worship of Christ is a poor plagiarism of the real thing.

Q: What action do you need to take against idols in your own life, art and work?

Q: What would be the consequences if you continued to worship these idols?

Q: How can you ask for God's help to root out idols in your life and become more like Christ?

Here's a prayer you might find helpful:

Dear God, help me to see the majesty of your Son Jesus so that I might see idols for what they really are. Help me to turn back to worshipping Jesus and keep my affections from worshipping others. In Jesus' name. Amen.

Q: What is the difference between healthy admiration and idolatry of an artist or idea?

Beyond Air Guitar

11. Making Culture

God's design for creative culture

Works of art equip us for action. And the range of actions for which they equip us is very nearly as broad as the range of human action itself. The purposes of art are the purposes of life. To envisage human existence without art is not to envisage human existence. Art—so often thought of as a way of getting out of the world—is man's way of acting in the world.

Nicholas Wolterstorff, theologian and writer[29]

Q: What words, pictures and ideas come to mind when you think of 'culture'?

Q: What role do you think Christians can play in making culture?

In the beginning God placed Adam in the Garden of Eden 'to work it and take care of it' (Gen 2:15). As we discussed in chapter 9, Adam's commission was for dominion over the creation and stewardship of that which God had created. This was both a privilege and a responsibility, and this commission continues today for all mankind. The Christian theologian and L'Abri Fellowship tutor Wim Rietkerk puts it like this: 'Mankind is called to develop this

world, to work in the fields of art, science, politics and economics. Christians should not withdraw from any of these areas. They should be active in all these area, because they are part of God's creation and God is more deeply present in all His work than we ever imagined.'[30]

In the Garden, Adam took from what God had created and reworked it to form new things. In cultivating the plants he took the soil, water and seed that God had created, ploughed the land and tended the crops to produce a harvest. In writing poetry about his wife he took the words, syntax and rhyme that God had first created and crafted them to form a new communication. At the beginning of creation Adam was making culture.

In a similar way we have been placed by God in the world today to work its ground and take care of it. For us who choose to become artists this means tending to the garden of the creative arts and media.

What is culture?

Let's take a moment to think about this question. What words, pictures and ideas come to mind when you think of 'culture'? When I ask this

29. From the opening chapter of his book Art in Action: Toward a Christian Aesthetic (Grand Rapids, MI: Eerdmans, 1980 / Carlisle: Paternoster, 2000).

30. From Wim Rietkerk, The Future Great Planet Earth (Goodbooks, 1989). Currently out of print. p. 21.

question at arts conferences there's usually someone who thinks it's funny to give the answer, 'Yogurt!' When you think about it, though, it's actually a really good response because the word 'culture' shares the same origins as the word 'cultivate'. 'Cultivate' means 'to grow a plant or crop, to bring multiplication or to improve or develop something'.[31] When you think of culture in the biological sense you might think of bacteria in a yogurt or cells that divide and multiply in a Petri dish, but this isn't entirely different from the processes of expanding and multiplying human culture.

By literal definition, to make culture is to take hold of something that already exists and rework it to bring multiplication, diversity, complexity, development or maturation. Culture can also mean other things.

Sometimes people think of culture with a capital 'C' that suggests art, music, literature and theatre. Culture can also be understood in terms of people and communities, their customs and rituals. Cultures can exist on a macro level: the national and international institutions of politics, economics and the arts; but it can also exist on a micro or local level such as town communities, families and peer groups.

Each of these definitions shares the common theme that culture is something that multiplies and develops through time. Culture is not static. It is always growing, dividing, multiplying and shaping the people or institutions who are a part of it.

Culture did not arrive flat-packed from Ikea

When God created the world it didn't arrive fully formed on day one but was cultivated through time. As we read the Genesis account, on day one God created the night and day but he returned later, on the fourth day, to make the sun and stars to enhance the night and day. On the second day God divided the sky from the waters but it wasn't until day five that he made the birds and fish to populate the skies and water. Similarly on day three God separated the sea from the land yet he waited until day six to create animals to inhabit the land and man to work on it and take care of it. God did not say, 'Let there be culture' but he laid a model for creation that involved separation then development of what he had made.

Adam reflected God's cultural process through taking from what

31. *Definition based on Encarta® World English Dictionary [North American Edition] © 2009 Microsoft Corporation. All rights reserved. Developed for Microsoft by Bloomsbury Publishing Plc..*

God had made, dividing it (literally, with the plough) and developing the ground. We might forget that there were only the beginnings of plant life in the Garden of Eden as 'no shrub of the field had yet appeared on the earth and no plant of the field had yet sprung up, for the Lord God had not sent rain on the earth and there was no man to work the ground' (Gen 2:5).

In order for the creation to continue being cultivated two actions were required of God and man. First, God had to send water to germinate the plants and, second, man had to work the ground. From this simple creative partnership God brought about the cultivation of the plants and set a precedent for making culture that would spread throughout every area of the creation and across the globe.

Like Adam, we take hold of what God has created and work it to bring multiplication and growth. We pray for a ground-swell of God's Spirit to germinate our efforts in the hope that through us he might bring water to the dry soil of the creative arts. For the writer it means taking words and cultivating them. For the designer it's starting with form, shape and ideas. For the painter the form and shape are focused into two

dimensions: colours and tones. We take from what God has first created and rework it to make something new, dividing colours, separating forms, returning to old words and developing them to make new modes of culture.

We are to bless the world

> God blessed them and said to them, 'Be fruitful and increase in number; fill the earth and subdue it. Rule over the fish of the sea and the birds of the air and over every living creature that moves on the ground.' (Gen 1:28)

At the beginning God gave Adam and Eve a mandate to bear fruit in the creation and increase in number. They were also to fill the earth and subdue it and, in so doing, demonstrate their authority over the rest of creation. As these instructions were given to the first human beings and have never been withdrawn, we must read them as applicable to ourselves today and not merely specific to life before the fall. These are instructions we shouldn't take lightly and they bear much significance for us who work in the arts. How do we work in the arts today? How can we take care of

God's creation through the making of art?

Genesis records that God blessed Adam and Eve as (or before) he gave them the instruction to bear fruit and increase. We have already seen, in chapter 5, that the word 'bless' can mean 'enlarge', which has something of a connection to the process of culturation (if we go with the idea that 'culture' is about multiplication and development). Just as God had authority over the first human beings and blessed them, so Adam and Eve, as those who bore the image of God, were to have dominion in creation and bless the world.

God gave them four instructions: be fruitful, increase in number, fill the earth and subdue it. Each instruction was related to the others, and the first three especially are connected.

'Be fruitful and increase in number; fill the earth …'

This wasn't just an instruction to have kids, although populating the earth was arguably a pressing need. We know that God's instruction to bear fruit applied to every area of the creation because Adam and Eve were also instructed to fill the whole earth.

'…and subdue it.'

Literally translated 'keep under', the word translated 'subdue' is used elsewhere in the Old Testament to describe the rule and authority of the Israelites over the surrounding nations (Num 32:22; Josh 18:1; 1 Chr 22:18). Whilst such strong language of domination and power might be uncomfortable hearing for contemporary ears, God's instruction is the same today: to have authority over the creation as God's custodians. Our rule should, however, bring blessing and not oppression. We are to 'be fruitful' in the creation. We are to bring 'increase'.

Christians are to bring blessing to the cultures in which God has placed us. We are to have dominion *and* responsibility. We are to work in the world *and* take care if it (cf. Gen 2:15); as Uncle Ben once said to Peter Parker in the classic Spider-Man comics, 'with great power comes great responsibility'.[32]

Power and responsibility

We are to be stewards of culture, pioneers, standard-bearers and initiators. For some of us that means making art that will have

32. *I'm grateful to Ed Mayhew who pointed out to me this quote was first attributed to Voltaire.*

influence on the national platform of the arts. For others it may require inspiring our children in making art around the kitchen table. Our cultural invention may be as simple as preparing a beautiful meal or showing hospitality. It may also involve teaching, critiquing, or curating exhibitions at the highest levels of arts society.

If we are to take care of the world, Christians also have collective responsibility in stewardship causes, such as environmental, political and economic action and campaigns against social injustice. It is not enough to sit back while others pick up the mantle. God has not lost interest in his creation even though it is subject to the fall, and as God continues to work in his creation through the power of his Spirit so should we, I believe, also be active.

In the arts we have a great opportunity to demonstrate God's concern for his world through the materials we choose and the ideas we raise in our work. A fashion designer may stand out for campaigning towards fairly traded clothing as well as appealing to the luxury market. A car designer can make a difference through exploring new possibilities in sustainable technologies and in the reduction of the environmental impact from fossil fuels and the apparent 'carbon footprint'. A film-maker can initiate awareness of forgotten or marginalized people groups in society. In each of these ways, and in many others, we can demonstrate the authority of Christ over every aspect of his creation. We can make obvious not just his rule but also his compassion for a broken world.

Q: What will it look like for you to 'work the ground' of the creative arts and take care of it through your work?

Q: How can you show authority and responsibility in your area of the creative arts or media?

Beyond Air
Guitar

12. Art and the New Creation

Art in the future and how it affects the present

I am making everything new.

Revelation 21:5

Q: What is the new creation? When does it start?

Q: What do you think life will be like for artists in heaven?

Great balls of fire and zombies rising from the ground: our view of the end times is all too influenced by films and popular culture. What will actually happen in the future? Will the earth be destroyed and all the art with it? Will there be new art? If so, who will be making it?

In these final two chapters of this part, we will tackle some of the big questions about life after Jesus returns and discuss how art we make now relates to what we will make then.

Spoilers

Since we are already citizens of the Kingdom of heaven, as Christians the work we make now should reflect, in some way, the heavenly reality of Christ's blessing and rule for ever. We could say that the art we make today acts a bit like a film trailer for a future release.

Just as a good map can help us plan for the road ahead, so an understanding of art in the future can help us make more sense of what priorities we should have as artists today. Paul writes, 'I press on towards the goal to win the prize for which God has called me heavenwards in Christ Jesus' (Phil 3:14) and it's good to have a sense of the finish line if we're going to run the race well.

Some things we know for sure about our life in the future: we know that Christ will return to judge (Rev 20:12,13); we know that he will establish a new heaven and a new earth (Rev 21:1); we know that those who trust in Christ will be with him for ever (Rev 21:3).

But there are other things that we can only speculate about. Some of the accounts in Revelation in particular are deliberately presented to us as pictures or poetic visions, but that is not to say that they are anything less than true impressions of future reality. I have tried to keep a level of measure as I've written this chapter and would caution that, whilst we get excited about the stuff we can look forward to with certainty, we try not to get too carried away with myths and rumours!

What do you mean, 'new creation'?

First, let's make a distinction between the new creation by God's Spirit today and the new heaven and new earth yet to come.

New creation now

God began his process of renewing his creation at the resurrection of Jesus who was the 'firstfruits' of the new creation, the first human being to be newly created (Col 1:15–20; 1 Cor 15:20). The new creation exists today in the lives of Christians, those who have been made new by God: 'Therefore, if anyone is in Christ, he is a new creation; the old has gone, the new has come!' (2 Cor 5:17).

Those who put their trust in Christ as their Lord and Saviour have been made new by his Spirit. Just as Christ rose from the grave, so will those who have his Spirit rise. There is a promise of new life in the future (Eph 1:13,14) but also of a new life now: 'For you have been born again, not of perishable seed, but of imperishable, through the living and enduring word of God' (1 Pet 1:23).

Paul writes to the Corinthians that we change from being 'natural' to 'spiritual' beings as our old identities, subject to the fall of nature, are replaced by God's Spirit: 'The body that is sown is perishable, it is raised imperishable; it is sown in dishonour, it is raised in glory; it is sown in weakness, it is raised in power; it is sown a natural body, it is raised a spiritual body' (1 Cor 15:42–44).

As fallen human beings we were born naturally into a sinful world and were perishing along with it. As we are born again through the Spirit the miracle of God transforms us into new beings who might look the same on the outside but who have now received a brand-new citizenship in God's Kingdom and are therefore guaranteed 'an inheritance that can never perish, spoil or fade' (1 Pet 1:4).

Paul also writes that 'where the Spirit of the Lord is, there is freedom' (2 Cor 3:17). Since the Spirit lives in us, our art should be a catalyst for green shoots of hope in a fallen world as God breathes freedom, blessing and renewal through the actions of his people.

New creation in the future

The renewing effects of the Spirit today are a promise of the future when God himself will fully renew his creation. God promises in the book of Revelation, 'I am making everything new!' (Rev 21:5).

In the future God will establish a new heaven and a new earth where Christians will live with Jesus and worship him for ever (Rev 21:3). This will be a heavenly reality for God's people on a renewed earth: a 'future kingdom' of God where Christ will establish his authority and blessing for ever. Whilst Christ's future Kingdom is evident throughout the whole sweep of Scripture we read about it especially in Isaiah 65 and 66, 1 Thessalonians, 1 Corinthians and the book of Revelation.

> I heard a loud voice from the throne saying, 'Now the dwelling of God is with men, and he will live with them. They will be his people, and God himself will be with them and be their God. He will wipe every tear from their eyes. There will be no more death or mourning or crying or pain, for the old order of things has passed away.' He who was seated on the throne said, 'I am making everything new!' (Rev 21:3–5)

God's future Kingdom will be incredible. In some ways the most vivid picture of the new creation is found in the resurrected body of Jesus. After he rose from the dead there were elements of his appearance that remained the same, yet he was also radically altered. On the road to Emmaus there was great drama as Jesus revealed himself to a few followers who at first didn't recognize his new form.

Jesus walked, talked and even ate a meal with his closest friends on the shores of Galilee. There will be much in the new earth that will be familiar to us, yet, at the same time, life will be very different. Not only the physical environment but also our own bodies will be renewed. Since Paul writes, 'The body that is sown is perishable; it is raised imperishable' (1 Cor 15:42) we know that our own bodies will no longer be subject to the perishable, dishonourable and weakening consequences of the fallen creation. It won't be possible for our bodies to become ill. We won't be tired after long evenings of painting.

The 'now' and the 'not yet' of the new creation

> We know that the whole creation has been groaning as in the pains of childbirth right up to the present time. Not only so, but we ourselves, who have the firstfruits of the

Spirit, groan inwardly as we wait eagerly for our adoption as sons, the redemption of our bodies. For in this hope we are saved. (Rom 8:22–24)

At the moment we live in the tension of life after the fall and before Jesus returns. Paul's imagery of childbirth is very striking: the creation itself groans with aches and pains as it looks forward to being fully renewed by Christ's Spirit, and we ourselves wait for him to return and wipe away every tear from our eyes when he sets up his new created order. Ask any mother how it feels to give birth and she will tell you about the pain.

Whilst the creation groans in labour pains we are comforted by 'tasters' of what life will be like in the future. Whenever we enjoy a good meal with friends, enjoy the beauty of the natural world or find work and art satisfying we are experiencing something of the goodness we'll enjoy in the new earth and we can get excited about what that reality will be like for us.

What will happen after Jesus returns?

Then I saw a new heaven and a new earth, for the first heaven and the first earth had passed away. (Rev 21:1)

When Jesus came to earth first time around it was to save. When he returns he will come to judge and make known his blessing and rule for ever.

Some Christians believe that the first creation will be completely destroyed. Verses in Peter's second letter certainly seem to indicate total destruction on first reading: 'the elements will be destroyed by fire, and the earth and everything in it will be laid bare' (2 Pet 3:10). Personally, I am convinced, along with many Bible commentators today, that the New International Version translation of this passage is not as helpful as it might be and that Peter's original Greek words speak more of renewal than complete annihilation.[33]

The idea of God renewing the earth is certainly more consistent with other Bible passages, such as Revelation 21:1, which describes the New Jerusalem coming down from heaven to earth rather than being founded on a brand-new planet somewhere else.

As God first declared the creation 'good' we know that he took pleasure from what he had made. Whilst the creation is now subject to the fall, and his creatures are rebellious

33. *As fire is an element, for example, we might ask how it can be destroyed by itself. It seems more likely that Peter is referring to a refiner's fire, as described elsewhere in the Bible (e.g. Mal 3:2): a fire that purifies rather than annihilates.*

towards him, there is *still* so much of the Creator's design evident within it. Not everything in the world is bad and surely God would not destroy that which he still finds good? When Martin Luther was asked what he would do if he knew that Christ would return the next day he replied, 'I would plant a tree.' Calvin, at least, presumed that something of the first creation would continue into the next.

As the creation mandate for mankind to have dominion over and responsibility for the creation still stands (and was renewed through Noah after the flood in Gen 9:1) we are to remain active in his world in every area, including the arts, and not see ourselves merely like the musicians who played on to muffle the sounds of the drowning as the *Titanic* sank to its inevitable end.

What stays and what goes?

Most of the questions about art and the future seem to boil down to the issue of continuity and discontinuity. What stays and what goes?

Will paintings we make today hang in the cloisters of Zion? Will Picasso's Cubist portraits make it to the new earth?

Whilst it is interesting to bounce these questions around there just isn't enough evidence in the Bible to give definite answers. I personally find it difficult to imagine God throwing out all the art made by his people, because he loves us and our art is an expression of our identity. Just as a father would want to keep his daughter's drawings so, I would suggest, God might want the art we make as spiritual children today to enjoy in the future.

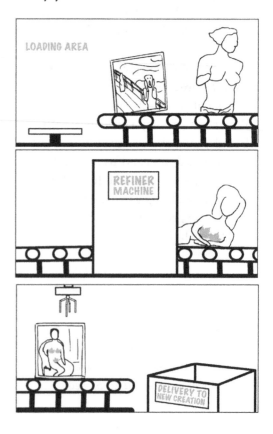

To be honest, however, I think these kinds of questions can be a bit of a distraction from the more important issues of the artist's character and godliness, which we know with certainty will make waves in the new creation.

Peter writes, 'Live such good lives among the pagans that, though they accuse you of doing wrong, they may see your good deeds and glorify God on the day he visits us' (1 Pet 2:12). Whilst the exact timing of God's 'visit' is not specified I don't think it stretches the text too far to suggest that the good artistic deeds we create (as art is an action) may be seen by others and lead them to glorify God on Christ's return. As Jesus himself said, 'let your light shine before men, that they may see your good deeds and praise your Father in heaven' (Matt 5:16).

We are also told that the 'deeds' of those who 'die in the Lord … will follow them' (Rev 14:13). Sometimes translated 'their good *works* will follow them' (my emphasis), this verse indicates that the artistic work we do today will make ripples in the Kingdom to come.

The actions we perform as Christians today are significant in the evangelism of others and will bear fruit in the new creation to come. Since the making of art is a relational activity it is fair, I think, to assume that the godliness of our art is as eternally significant in the Kingdom of God as is every other action we perform or words we share.

What will art be like on the new earth?

If you are a Christian and an artist there is much to look forward to in the new earth. God's word promises an abundance of creative art including music (Rev 14:2,4), architecture (Isa 65:21,22; Rev 21) and new clothes (Rev 19:8), which are just a taster of the wider culture for the arts we will experience. The myth that we will all simply sit around on clouds getting bored as we strum harps in the future new creation is completely unfounded. Far from it: we will work, work well, and finally find our creative endeavours completely satisfying.

Imagine that you have been saving up for months to book a big holiday and you go online to check out the flights and hotels. As you get excited about what the holiday might be like you naturally check out a few websites that tell you about your destination or you pop down to the travel agent's to pick up a few holiday brochures. Imagining your final destination is part of the enjoyment of the holiday. In the same way, it would be pretty stupid not to read or think about what life will be like for us in the future on a new earth, which will be far greater than any city break or week in the sun we could ever imagine today. There are some things we know and some things we can only speculate about, but let's start with what we know with certainty and can get really excited about.

In the future there *will* be art …

… Without sin

> Behold, I will create
> new heavens and a new earth,
> The former things will
> not be remembered
> nor will they come to mind.
> (Isa 65:17)

On the new earth there will be no more sin. God will not allow us to rebel against him and corrupt the creation around us any more. Similarly, 'There will be no more death or mourning or crying or pain, for the old order of things has passed away' (Rev 21:4). Even the memory

of sin, according to Isaiah, will be a thing of the past (although this raises other questions of continuity and memory that we will discuss below).

With the problem of sin removed we will be able to make art without jealousy, rivalry or selfish ambition. We will visit a gallery and be genuinely pleased for the achievements of other artists. Notions of success and failure will be changed for ever, as everything we do will bring glory to God.

… That satisfies

> They will build houses
> and dwell in them;
> they will plant vineyards
> and eat their fruit.
> No longer will they build
> houses and others live in them,
> or plant and others eat.
> For as the days of a tree,
> so will be the days of my people;
> my chosen ones will long enjoy
> the works of their hands.
> (Isa 65:21,22)

In the future there will be work. When we work with our hands (*arte factum*) it will bring great satisfaction to us and to those around us every time. Isaiah's words are the language of home, security and rest.

Revelation describes a perfectly designed city, dazzling with jewel-encrusted buildings and gold streets as transparent as glass. Zion is a garden city with a river flowing through its heart from the throne of Jesus himself. Revelation describes the city coming down from heaven, which suggests a form of completion, but there are many metaphors and symbols at work in this image. Will some Christians perhaps work in the continued construction and development of the capital city of the new earth?

Adam partnered God in founding culture and making art in the Garden of Eden; Bezalel carried out the work for the tabernacle; and we create and make new culture today that gives glory to God. God creates with his people for his glory and their satisfaction.

... For eternity

> Since, then, you have been raised with Christ, set your hearts on things above, where Christ is seated at the right hand of God. Set your minds on things above, not on earthly things. (Col 3:1–2)

Will we get bored on the new earth? Rather than thinking of *eternity* as linear, going on and on and on without end, think of it as a qualitative term that describes the rule and blessing of Christ in the new creation; *eternity* can be seen as the goodness of God that extends without end.

When we think about the eternal qualities of art we make today we should worry less about its longevity and more about its *goodness*. In the future all art will be 'good'. We will sing, dance, paint, sculpt, design and write in a way that pleases us, the audience and the Lord alike.

Those are aspects of the new earth we can look forward to with certainty, but there are also possibilities we can only speculate about, though not without justification. The pictures the Bible gives us for the future are often symbols or signs of real things to come.

In the future there *may* be art affected by ...

... New concepts of time

Consider, for example, making time-based art when the universe will continue for ever. You could make a film that lasted for millennia and no one would get bored. No deadlines to meet. No burning the midnight oil. No stealing of time to catch up with the backlog of work.

In the future there will be a new beginning but there will be no end. We won't be comparing ourselves with others in the art history of the new earth because they will be living right there with us. A masterpiece may be started and completed in a day or be developed for centuries. We will be able to make truly amazing work and time will no longer be our enemy.

… New ways of making

In the future the laws of physics may be renewed. We get a hint of a new physical reality in the resurrected body of Jesus, which was no longer subject to nature but appeared through walls in the upper room, ascended up to heaven and was recognizable yet foreign at the same time.

In the future we will no longer be subject to the fallen condition of nature. In the beginning God designed us to have dominion over everything in the world yet the creation has mastered us when we should have had

authority over it. The days make us tired, ploughing the soil breaks our backs, we work all day on a drawing and we get blisters. None of these issues will be a problem for us in the future.

The resurrected Jesus ate breakfast with his disciples by the shores of Galilee. In the future we will eat and share meals together. In Revelation we read about a great banquet at the wedding of Jesus and his bride, the church. There will be food in the future kingdom. There will be mealtimes and drinking. For this reason the Christian shouldn't deny the simple pleasures of preparing a meal or eating with friends. It is not 'worldly' to go out for dinner with your husband or wife or throw a good dinner party. In fact, since eating together is part of our eternal future, I could suggest we get in a bit of practice now!

Since there is no pain in the future we might ask if there will be any friction, as the same physical laws responsible for blisters and grazes also allow us to paint, sculpt and strum the guitar. How will we bow a string, press on a typewriter or scribble in a notebook? In a similar way, in a future without decay and destruction, how will we cook, process film and garden? Will there be compost in the new earth?

As God's people we will not be subject to the laws of creation but will have a fully renewed dominion over them. We could speculate that friction will no longer be our master but that we will control it and therefore there will be no more blistering and bruising when we work or decay and destruction when we are finished unless this is important to our creative process.

... New ways of seeing

As the focus shifts from ourselves to the glory of Christ we will no longer struggle to make art for the sole glory of God. Books like this won't be needed!

In the future there will arguably also be no darkness as we know it, because the light of Christ will illuminate the whole creation.

... New notions of 'completeness'

Our notions of 'perfection' and 'completeness' will be transformed as we will be satisfied with work made in a day as much as with that laboured over for centuries. As many of our creative processes today depend on dynamic tensions there is every

likelihood that there will be dynamism and tension in the future. We will work with ideas and paradoxes, we will grapple with work though not grow tired, and there will always be new skills to learn and questions to explore. Just as today the new creation is not static so in the future we can speculate that there will be creative tensions for us to work from and be inspired by.

Personally, I am looking forward to finally getting round to learning the piano. In the future kingdom I may not be able to play like Mozart after one lesson but I will be satisfied with what I have achieved and will genuinely give thanks to God for others who can play better than me.

What is 'perfection' anyway? To some, a project is complete when it is perfect but there will always be more work for us to do in the future new creation, just as we will also be lacking nothing and will not need to work to sustain the world.

... New stories to tell

In a future without pain, suffering or grieving what will we make art about? Will we remember the sorrow of the past or will we simply make art about being happy? We have already considered Isaiah's words, 'The former things will not be remembered nor will they come to mind' (Isa 65:17), but what exactly will we forget?

When the resurrected Christ appeared to his disciples in the upper room he invited Thomas to feel his scars; even the resurrected body of Christ contained a memory of past suffering. On the throne at the centre of the city of Zion sits the Lamb of God (Rev 14) who was the atonement sacrifice for sins. We will worship the Lamb, rejoice around him and remember what he has done for us. This memory, at least, will be at the centre of all we do in the capital city of the new earth.

The stories we tell will surely be rich in tension and even paradox. We will tell stories of the Lamb who was slain yet had victory over death. We may remember rebellion in the first creation and praise God for the glory of the new. Most of us will have tasted death yet we will also have experienced the wonderful transformation of the resurrected life.

Not clichéd or kitsch, not twee or dull: we will tell the stories of creation, fall, redemption and renewal, stories of people, places, love lost and found, the magnificence of the mountains and the innocence of children, of Christ's rule and blessing over all creation. In short, we will continue to tell all the stories of the gospel.

Art in the new creation now

Today, as new *spiritual* beings we have been transformed from our old lives and brought into the new Kingdom of Christ's rule and blessing for ever. When Christians make art it should be the best news the arts world has ever heard. Our art should be dynamic and redemptive, reflecting the creative energy of the Creator himself and the eternal qualities of the Kingdom to come. Understanding how we will make art in the future gives us a model for working and creating today, perhaps not in form but certainly in principle as we look now to make art that is 'good', is satisfying and has eternal significance.

As we have already discussed elsewhere in this book (although perhaps not made clear until now), when we make art as a blessing to the world we are making the art of the new creation. When we create under the Lordship of Christ we are reflecting his rule today but also proclaiming his blessing in the future. When we pray 'thy Kingdom come' over the creative arts, we are asking for the Lord's rule to be evident today as well as to see his name glorified in the arts of the future.

Q: How do these models for art in the future influence the art that you make today?

Q: What are some of the practical implications for you and your work from these reflections on the new creation?

13. A Sight for Sore Eyes

On beauty and redemption

*How beautiful on the mountains
are the feet of those who bring good news,
who proclaim peace,
who bring good tidings,
who proclaim salvation,
who say to Zion,
'Your God reigns!'*

Isaiah 52:7

Q: What words, pictures and ideas come to mind when you hear the word 'beauty'?

Q: What do you understand by the word 'redemption'? How can art be redemptive in a fallen world?

What is beauty?

'Beauty' is a noun taken from the Latin word *bellus* which quite simply translates as 'pretty', but the origins of the concept of beauty as we understand it today are arguably found in Ancient Greece. Although the Ancient Greeks had no concept of beauty as we understand it today, they displayed a strong concern for formal aesthetics as demonstrated by the proportion, symmetry and geometry of their architecture, craft and design which became the foundation for modern concepts of visual aesthetics.

In the classical Greek period the closest concept to beauty was *kallos,* which means symmetry or 'good proportion', but another idea began to emerge several centuries later known as *horaios,* which means 'hour' or 'of the hour'. This was the idea of something or someone who was 'of the time' or contemporary. A bowl of fruit, for example, was *horaios* if it was ripe to eat. A young woman who had come of age was *horaios* because she was 'of her hour'.

'Beauty' is an idea or an ideal. It is something we aspire to have. It is generally regarded as a good thing; it is a compliment to be called 'beautiful' and we like to surround ourselves with beautiful things at home, such as fine art, food and clothes.

We often hear the saying, 'Beauty is in the eye of the beholder', which suggests that beauty is subject to personal tastes and preferences. The pictures, people and places that *you* think are beautiful might not be ones that *I* think are beautiful. 'Beauty' is subject to personal and cultural variations such as where we're from, our gender, what we're used to and what our friends and family think.

Most cultures seem to have an understanding of the concept of 'beauty' even if we don't agree on what is actually 'beautiful'. We all seem to agree that there is beauty in the created world: in the colours of the setting sun and the fragrance of the flowers. 'Beauty' might be subject to personal and cultural tastes, but is there also a sense of universal, even absolute, beauty?

Beauty in the Bible

As we read the creation story in Genesis 1 there is a sense of good proportion and symmetry as God creates through division and multiplication (as discussed in chapter 8): he separated the waters from the land then instructed Adam and Eve to take care of the land, bear fruit and increase in number.

In Genesis 2:9, God declares the trees to be 'pleasing to the eye' and not just 'good for food'. From the beginning it is clear that God is concerned with the aesthetic dimension to his creation as well as how it functions.

We have already seen concern for formal aesthetics in the design for the tabernacle and we see the same thing in the majestic temple of Solomon, which housed music, incense, sculpture, wall sculpture and textiles that pleased God and even incorporated two pillars that were finished expensively in bronze (1Ki 7:15).

The Bible demonstrates God's interest in the way things look, but it also describes beauty in another sense, a greater concern that reflects the eternal qualities of the created order and not just the way things appear. The prophet Isaiah said, 'How beautiful on the mountains are the feet of those who bring good news' (Isa 52:7), words repeated by the apostle Paul in Romans 10. In the Bible, beauty is related to redemption.

Did Isaiah and Paul have a foot fetish? Was there something particularly attractive about the prophets' feet? The feet of the evangelist are beautiful because they carry upon them the good news that Jesus Christ is Lord and Saviour. It is the beauty of the message that gives beauty to the messenger, not the dimensions of their feet!

In the book of Revelation, the apostle John describes a great wedding feast for Christ and his bride, the church, at which 'Fine linen, bright and clean, was given her to wear' (Rev 19:8). John describes how the beautiful linen of the bride stands for the righteous acts of the saints, illustrating God's love for beautiful deeds and not just for beautiful artefacts. In a similar way in Proverbs 31 the wife of noble character is noted for a beauty that runs deeper than her outward appearance and reflects instead the godliness of her manner.

What is redemption?

The word 'redeem' means 'to buy back'. If we consider 'redemption' with a lower-case 'r', so to speak, we might think of something like a chair or picture frame that has been restored to its former beauty or a pawned engagement ring that has been bought back, both of which would be 'beautiful' acts for a friend.

As Christians, we also think about 'redemption' with an upper-case 'R': the redemptive acts of Jesus in buying back all things to God through his death and resurrection. As Paul writes to the Colossians, 'God was pleased to have all his fulness dwell in him, and through him to reconcile to himself all things, whether things on earth or things in heaven, by making peace through his blood, shed on the cross' (Col 1:19,20). This was the ultimate redemptive act that reflects the beauty of Christ and his deep love for his bride, the church and all creation, as 'Christ died ... once for all' (1 Pet 3:18) so that everyone might have the opportunity to be restored to God. Whilst Christ is the Redeemer of all things he also sent his Spirit to those who follow him so that they might demonstrate his redemption through their lives, words and actions. As the Spirit of Christ dwells in us, we can ask for the redemptive power of his Spirit to inspire our creative acts. We can pray that our art will bear fruit in the world and demonstrate the light of Christ where there is darkness.

As Christians we have the possibility of performing redemptive acts and making redemptive art because the power of Christ's Spirit is in us. This isn't some kind of magical power or superhuman weirdness, such as walking through walls or turning lead into gold; we demonstrate glimmers of hope for a new creation because Christ's Spirit is in us and 'and where the Spirit of the Lord is, there is freedom' (2 Cor 3:17).

We get a sense of redemptive art in the parables of Jesus in which a man comes across a precious pearl and sells everything he owns to possess it, or finds beautiful artefacts in the most unexpected of places and sells everything he owns so that he can buy this treasure (Matt 13).

The beauty of Christ's redemption is also demonstrated in his miracles, such as that performed at the wedding at Cana, when Jesus turned water into wine. The new creation is like a fine-tasting wine, with so much flavour, colour and vitality compared with the bland fallen creation.

Redemptive beauty in art

Just as Jesus used parables to describe the treasures of God's Kingdom and miracles to demonstrate its blessing, so our art can point towards the beauty of Christ's redemption, demonstrating his blessing to the world and the values of his new creation.

Wherever art demonstrates light in the darkness, hope in despair, renewal in destruction or the promise of rest at the end of the long, weary road, it reflects a glimmer of Christ's redemption. Wherever death is exposed as the enemy, wherever sin and its consequences are battled against, wherever God's justice is made known, wherever the compassion of Christ is displayed, wherever the Lordship of Jesus is illustrated as reality: in all these ways, works of art can show how the Spirit of Christ is active through the redemption of the Son.

Our task is to be faithful to Christ's instruction to work well in his creation and take care of it, but also to work towards the reality of the new creation to come when God will make *everything* new. The renewal of the world can happen only through the power of God, but for us who serve him and make art for his sake, there is the possibility of demonstrating redemption and being redemptive in our art and actions.

This is the hope of many Christian artists and designers around the world and is, of course, best illustrated through real-life studies, not just described in principle. As we

head into the third major discussion
of this book, it's my hope that the
redemptive beauty of Christ will be
demonstrated through the lives and
work of those who are featured in
the following pages and who seek to
serve Christ and make him known
in the arts, not just in principle but
through demonstration.

Q: What is 'beautiful' and
'redemptive' in your own art?
What needs to change or
develop?

Q: Take a few moments to list a
few works of art that demonstrate
the redemptive beauty of Christ's
Spirit in the fallen creation. How
are they redemptive? How do
they make a difference to the
world?

Q: In this chapter we have
discussed beauty in relation to
redemption but said nothing of
the virtues of ugliness. What is
'ugliness' and how can it reflect
something of how God sees the
world?

The Stories We Tell

An interval

Hanging on his every word the crowd drew closer, lingering under the lazy afternoon sun in the hope of more. *Give us another one about a wedding. Give us the one about the net. The one about the treasure. The story of the pearl.* His stories would ignite sparks in the hearts of his audience, warming some who drew near and burning those who wished to escape. He would say, 'He who has ears, let him hear' (Matt 13:43) and 'Don't you understand?' (Mark 4:13), never pandering to the wants of his audience but ministering to their needs. He teased them, enticed them, got under their skin until his stories jagged like barbed wire in the flesh that wouldn't let go until their thirsty ears had taken their fill.

When it came to telling stories, there were few who could match Jesus.

So what stories will *we* tell? What ideas will we explore? What questions will we put out there?

Authentic stories

Every story reflects a worldview and ours can begin with the truth of why the world is as it truly is. As Paul writes to the Philippians, 'whatever is true, whatever is noble, whatever is right, whatever is pure, whatever is lovely, whatever is admirable—if anything is excellent or praiseworthy—think about such things' (Phil 4:8).

How do we write what is true? How do we paint what is noble, or perform what is right, pure, lovely or admirable? Do we daydream about safe pastures and avoid stories of wolves? No, in our art we nurture a Christian hope that will never perish, spoil or fade. That means a story of hope that engages the fallen world on its own terms but that points beyond what is seen to that which is genuine, real and authentic—to the gospel.

Stories about people

Since God made people in his own image we know that human beings are of great interest to God. We can tell stories about people. Every person has a story to tell, and what better stories are there than those about the struggles, joys, tragedies, triumphs, laughs, regrets, hopes, endurance and dignity of people made in the image of God?

Creation stories

Since Christians know something about why the world was created, we can tell the stories of creation: how it was created, who created it and why it has become fallen and broken. When God created the world he said, 'It is good.' In our art we can point towards the wonder of God's creation. The Christian can explore the themes of the created order: how the world works, the landscape, the human form or the difference between created humans and the other creatures of the world.

Fallen stories

As Christians, our tendency can be to put a cheerful chorus at the end of a depressing song to say that everything is going to be all right, but what if it's not? What if we need to reflect, even for a moment, on the fallen reality that the world is broken and there will be pain, grief and tears?

As Christians we can tell stories of the fall because we know that death is not the end. We portray the beauty of the world without a sentimental or kitsch gloss *because* we know that the creation is groaning and awaiting renewal.

Stories of justice

Some stories take a sentimental view of justice: the bad guys get away but we all have a good laugh about it. Other stories take a balanced view of justice: the good guys win the day and the bad guys get their come-uppance. What is God's way of dealing out justice? God's justice is neither sentimental nor balanced. Instead, God's justice is *complete*.

Can you imagine a story in which the bad guys get off scot-free and the good guy pays the price for the crime, or in which the worst possible outcome is only a veil to disguise the drama of the master plan? This is God's story of justice.

Stories that arise in the moment

We can tell stories about the past and commemorate important events; we are in culture, bringing something of an incarnate Christianity to the world around us. We tell the stories of the future and speak relevance to our times.

Art can be an action of hope: it can bring order and rhythm to the chaos. Art can be an action of love: it can bring people together and stimulate positive discussion. Art can be an action of peace, renewal and hope. Art can challenge, provoke, redefine and subvert, offer new possibilities and horizons, stimulating growth in the lives both of those who make it and of those whose thirsty ears are listening.

Introduction

I have always found that the most helpful advice on living for Christ in the arts comes from those who make art and have spent years trying to work out how best to do it. Having spent a little time in this book considering what the Bible says about art and design we now turn to those who actually practise in these fields.

This collection of interviews attempts to offer a broad application of biblical principles over a variety of creative fields. The advice is practical and the situations real.

Some interviews took place using email, some were conducted over the phone and others were recorded live over lunch. They reveal the true stories of artists' and designers' experiences after graduation. Most are working full-time in the arts. Some are heading that way. All are serious about serving Christ with integrity in the creative arts and industries.

14. NORMAN STONE

On grafting a career in film-making, where to draw the line and the value of collaboration

Award-winning director Norman Stone has directed and produced TV and film since 1975. Employed as the BBC's youngest producer/director, he initially worked in the *Everyman* documentary strand and established his career in 1984 when he invented, developed and directed *Shadowlands* for BBC1. This gained him two BAFTA awards, an International Emmy, and the Prague D'Or for Best Director.

Stone has directed a number of top TV dramas including two *Miss Marple*s and two *Catherine Cookson*s, winning another International Emmy for *The Black Velvet Gown*, which starred Bob Peck and Janet McTeer. Other awards include a BAFTA for the *Omnibus* special on the life of Dudley Moore, *After the Laughter,* an Andrew Cross Award for best documentary of the year for *The Tartan Pimpernel* and a Golden Remi for his first feature film, *Man Dancin'*, which he created and directed in his home town of Glasgow. His most recent work includes the film documentary *The Narnia Code* and a film chronicling the lives of the King James Bible translators.

This interview took place over the phone during a break in editing.

AG: Hello, Norman. You've just come back from filming?

NS: I've just come back from filming and I've been editing all this week. Every hour that God sends us we're working here.

AG: What's the current project? Can I ask?

NS: Yeah, of course. It's a ninety-minute drama documentary on the King James Bible. It's going to be 400 years old next year [2011] and I wanted to tell the story of the people who were connected to that translation rather than give a lecture on the stuff. It's a dramatic story and we have some interesting people involved. John Rhys-Davies is involved with this one. Most people know him as Gimli the dwarf in *Lord of the Rings* but he's actually a very large man in real life. I don't know why they got him to play a dwarf. [laughs]

AG: He was in some of the *Indiana Jones* films. He's huge. He'd have been better as a troll. He's a big-name actor, too. Do you find that you generally get the people you want to work with you?

NS: He's excellent to work with. Right from the start. No, I can't quite pick and choose everything I want. I don't think anyone really can. But it comes in seasons. After the

BAFTA awards the phone rang quite a lot and I was able to take on some interesting work that I really wanted to do. There was a bit of a gap after that but the Narnia stuff opened up good things again, and, of course, *Florence Nightingale.*

AG: What makes for an interesting project?

NS: Something with heart. I like to tell stories that have a lot of heart. Sometimes they're stories that are closer to an overtly Christian message, like the recent *Narnia* documentary, but really I don't want to be typecast as the 'Christian' director and have worked hard to avoid that association. God is interested in all stories and the Christian involvement isn't limited to stories about things that just seem Christian. I was asked to make this film about the 400th anniversary of the King James Bible and it was the people surrounding the translating and printing of this hugely influential version of the Bible that really make the story come alive. It's a story about people, not just a documentary about the Bible. They were extraordinary people and I think their story needs to be told. The film looks at what was happening in politics at the time and there's an explosive part involving

Guy Fawkes. It's going to be a great film. But I've also been asked to make films on lots of other things. I was asked to make a film about the Baha'i faith and I explained to them that I was an evangelical Christian and I would be coming from that position. I was very clear about what stance I would take and they still wanted me to be involved in the project, so sometimes you never know. I've worked in TV dramas and worked with some really super people. Some have been Christian but most have not.

AG: Your portfolio covers a lot of genres, from pop videos to documentaries about Florence Nightingale, and C. S. Lewis to Miss Marple episodes, and even adaptations from Dostoevsky. You're probably best known for films like *Man Dancin'* and your early work on *Shadowlands,* the story of C. S. Lewis which is now really big.

NS: Really that's following the lead from Lewis, who wrote about everything. There were the *Narnia* books but he also wrote science fiction and other children's stories as well as the Christian books. He showed how God is interested in all these stories and he wrote, of course, extremely well. He put in the hard graft. He crafted his words. It was

a privilege to be involved with the early days of *Shadowlands* and for the first film, and of course it took off and they made first the stage play and then the big Hollywood movie version.

AG: It's still running in the West End today.

NS: Yes, I think his story is a story that many people related to and he brought belief in God to a human level through his general writing as well as in his books.

AG: Did he set the benchmark?

NS: He certainly showed us how it could be done. He was an extraordinary Christian man.

AG: Who else has been an inspiration to you? Who helped you and encouraged you as a Christian in the early stages of your career?

NS: Rookmaaker. John Stott. To some extent, Schaeffer. Meryl Doney. My old friend Steve Turner continues to do good things and is always inspiring. There was a group of us back in the early days of the Arts Centre Group that met regularly to work together, discuss things and critique one another's work. Many of them have gone on to do some very interesting work and become well known in their own right. We even put on shows occasionally. That was a lot of fun and very influential in forming a sense of community for me in the early days that I'm still grateful for now. I still keep in touch with many of them. We used to go away for weekends together. We performed in Edinburgh at the Festival. There's no substitute for that kind of collaboration.

AG: What made the group work?

NS: The thing is, we were honest with each other about our work because we knew it mattered and we knew it mattered to God. One of our group had been offered a huge part in a West End play (which was great) ... but he would have to swear and play a very evil character indeed. He was worried about whether he should do it and what was the right Christian thing to do. At the time it was really only Rookmaaker who was writing for Christians in the arts and elsewhere the perceived wisdom was that a Christian shouldn't really take that kind of part if it was ever offered. However, this young actor also said that the overall message of the play was incredibly redemptive, even though he would have to play what was undoubtedly the worst character he'd ever come

across. I remember we all had a great discussion over an open Bible, and prayed about this very real and practical situation. I think he went on to play the part, but we all benefited greatly from having to think it through.

In the end, it's all about choice and responsibility. I can't tell you what work you should or shouldn't take but I can tell you that, as a Christian, you do have both the freedom and the responsibility to choose one thing over the other. You just have to be a bit careful and prayerful and be honest to the God of truth and love. You don't need to take the part if it's damaging to you or to others. You don't need to take the work. You can make a choice and be responsible in that choice.

AG: For many of our graduates the pressure is, they're skint and need any work they can get.

NS: Yes, that's true, and that's the difficult issue, but if you have others around you who you trust they can help you make these decisions. The situation might not be as desperate as you think. Of course, it might be the competition is very fierce but you are still good at what you do. It might be that you need to train harder. It might be that you shouldn't be in acting, and that's a difficult thing to admit, but it might be better for you if you just get out and do something else.

AG: For many of our students the old-chestnut question is, what makes success? How do you know when you're being successful?

NS: Obedience ... it's as simple as that. You work hard. You put in the hours. You pray for the opportunities and you keep plugging away at it. It's being obedient to God that really counts. God is more interested in our obedience to him than he is in any awards we have won or how famous we are. Having friends around you who can help you see what's what is very helpful in this and I've been privileged to have some good people around me who've helped me make some of the tougher work decisions that would affect other things in my life, like my family and friends. But it's being faithful to what God asks of us that's important. To our families. To our church. To ourselves. To him.

15. ROBERT ORCHARDSON

On belief in the arts, utopian futures and new sculpture

Robert Orchardson is a London-based sculptor. After studying at Goldsmiths College Robert was a Bloomberg New Contemporaries 2005 exhibitor and has subsequently exhibited in Berlin, Rome and across the UK. His major public commissions include *Nexus* for British Land Plc and *The Substance of Things Unseen* for the Economist Plaza, both in London.

This interview took place as an email conversation.

AG: Robert, what projects do you have on the go? What's hanging on your studio wall right now?

RO: At the moment I have work in a couple of exhibitions—one in Germany at a gallery in a place called Schwäbisch Hall, the other in Nottingham Castle Art Gallery.

The German one is my work alongside a German artist who made hard-edge abstraction in the 1970s. The show in Nottingham is a show curated by the artist-run space Moot, as part of The Contemporary Art Society's 100th anniversary programme. It is an interesting exhibition. Moot selected several drawings from the city collection and invited various artists to make work which 're-presented' each drawing somehow. I was given drawings by the artist Liliane Lijn. They were preparatory drawings for sculptures—technical diagrams, really. I liked the fact that the drawings were not end-products, so to speak—more carriers for an idea or working models. I wanted to play upon this aspect of the works and I made some precarious-looking sculptures inspired by easels, or slightly odd drawing boards, upon which the drawings rested. I wanted to liberate them from being stuck in a frame or pinned down behind glass when I don't think they were ever made for that. They seemed more at home on something like a drawing board. It is nice to make work which is not just about my work in isolation, but which enters into some sort of a dialogue with another artist.

What else have I got on the go at the moment? I have some works on paper in the studio, which I might put into a small exhibition someone I know is organizing. They are part of a series of works where I print directly onto pages from *National Geographic* magazines. The works are kind of inspired by the collages of architectural groups like Superstudio.

I am also trying to develop work for a large solo exhibition due to take place next year, as well as some other possible projects that may or may not happen.

AG: You have described your work as having a kind of optimism to it, even a spirituality that draws from your interest in modernist and futurist architecture and design. There's also a connection to science fiction and ideas of utopia and a better future. How did you become interested in these ideas? How do they connect together in the work?

RO: Where to start … there's quite a few things there. There's a verse in the Bible [Eccl 3:11] which says God

'has set eternity in the hearts of men'. I've always found this an incredible idea, the contrast between finite and infinite, and in retrospect, consideration of this has been a central aspect of my artwork for a long time, even if I didn't realize it for a while or necessarily set out to do so.

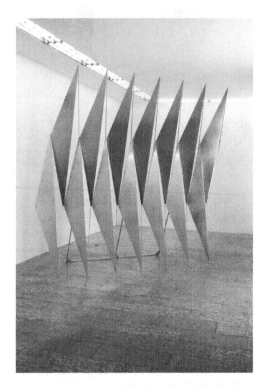

At college I found myself making paintings which drew on an interest I had in the so-called space race of the 1950s and 60s. I wasn't entirely sure what interested me in this period at first but gradually understood it to be something of the sense of potential that it embodied ... the space race seemed to encapsulate that sensibility well. It was simultaneously fuelled by, and also itself in turn fuelled, an ambitious optimism, while also contributing to the apocalyptic threat of the cold war. Either way, people were acutely interested in what this unknown future held. J. G. Ballard put it well when he said of this period that 'for the first time the future was a better key to the present than was the past'.

So there was this tension between utopian and dystopian futures. These things filtered into the cultural consciousness, and had an impact on society in general and, of course, the work of artists, designers, film-makers and so on. I began to make work which was inspired by some of this stuff, but came to understand that what interested me about these influences was their underlying exploration of ways in which we might look beyond our immediate situation, considering that which seems unknown. Over time I have expanded the range of cultural flotsam and jetsam which surfaces in my work, helping me consider these things, but I think an underlying interest in a tension between the here and now and ideas of some kind of unknown 'other' remain relevant and pivotal to what I make.

I'm not sure how much that answers your question, though!

AG: There was an interesting show at Nottingham Contemporary a few months ago, dealing with visions for the future under Communism and the space race between America and the USSR in the 60s. It was a fascinating show—*Star City*—and it brought your work to mind. Did you see it? To me, it demonstrated something of this human longing for another, better world, something 'other', as you describe it—but something engineered through the invention and triumph of mankind rather than anything to do with God's work through new creation or what we might believe as Christians.

There was a sense of pride and hope for the future, shared by many, under these regimes. It seemed acceptable, you were encouraged, to believe in things that were greater than yourself, almost like a religion in itself. This seems to contrast dramatically with contemporary, Western ideology that is suspicious of institutional belief systems, where there is cynicism about the future and where we are encouraged to believe in self.

How free are we to deal with issues of belief in art today? Do you see an openness in the contemporary arts to discuss issues of faith, or is that a taboo subject?

RO: Yeah, I saw the exhibition in Nottingham … though it really was a flying visit, but it looked like an interesting show. The cinema that was made to show a remake of the opening part of Andrei Tarkovsky's *Solaris* seemed interesting, but, like I say, I wasn't really able to do the show any justice as I was dashing through.

But sure, I think you are right: there are certainly overlaps in terms of where the show was coming from and things that my work has considered. I have quite a few bits and pieces of memorabilia from that time, like old *Life* magazines or newspaper articles that commemorate the moon landings, and there is a tangible sense of 'belief' and wonder at what humankind might achieve. People were beginning to engage with a new sort of sublime experience. Interestingly, though, this seemed to reach a peak with the moon landings—obviously there were lots of reasons for the momentum to slow down, not least financial, but perhaps interest waned once that which once seemed out of reach was no longer inaccessible.

We now live in different times, and I wonder if belief is harder for many people. I wonder if we have developed a kind of cynicism due in part to the failed aspirations of things like the space programme. I guess my work tries to revisit some of those moments of aspiration— whether it be in relation to conquest of space, or the sense of hope cultivated by modernist ideals filtering into architecture or design. I'm not trying to propose that we should necessarily regain feelings of aspiration in relation to these things, but I am interested in considering those moments of promise before they became tainted by failure—'freeze-framing fantasy', as Michelle Cotton described it, 'exploring the spiritual and conceptual investment in the formal language of the modern' [exhibition text for *Crystal Peaks*, S1 Artspace, 2005]. In terms of discussing belief in contemporary art I am not sure that it's a taboo as such. I think there is scope, indeed, need, for this; however, I also think there is a commonly held preconception by many that faiths promote redundant philosophy. This can perhaps lead to work that engages with traditional notions of faith in a negative way, without really being open to reconsidering their relevance with open minds.

AG: You've shown work in some very interesting spaces, such as Glasgow's CCA, Wilkinson Gallery in London, Ben Kaufmann in Berlin, Monitor in Rome, and site-specific installations such as the Economist Plaza in London and the *Nexus* project. There are many artists who would kill for those kinds of projects. How do you make opportunities for your work? Do you go out of your way to find them or do the opportunities come to you?

RO: I am fortunate enough that these things have pretty much come to me ... I am terrible at self-publicity and these projects seem to happen more 'in spite of', and less 'because of', me!

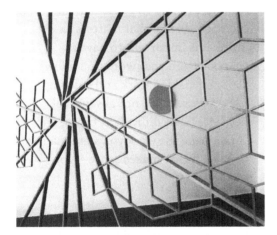

AG: I remember you saying at an Interface event that you tend not to run the gauntlet of the private views or go chasing after galleries. Do you think the better strategy is to make the work as good as possible and let it speak for itself? Does one project well done open up a possibility for the next?

RO: I don't think there is any kind of formula you can apply to these things ... yes, I do think that it is of course more important to focus on making good work. Though, having said that, there are some artists who are very good at 'working a crowd' and knowing the right people. It is probably true that if you are on people's radars, so to speak, you are more likely to be invited to be involved in projects that come up, so if you are good at getting out there and making your work known there will be some curators or collectors who will like what they see. I think it is a mixture of things though. You have to be doing something right if people consistently find the work interesting, but I'm not sure that just making good work is enough—I think you need to have some measure of willingness to be exhibiting your work and allowing it to be seen as well. As you do that and as people start to engage with your work, I have frequently found that many projects lead to other things.

AG: One last question. This book is aimed at students and recent graduates who are trying to work out the transition between student life and surviving after art college. If you could meet yourself again as a recent graduate from art college, what advice would you want to give?

RO: There's no one-size-fits-all answer; each person's situation is different. I guess one of the things I quickly realized once I left college was how much I'd taken for granted while at college ... the studio space, workshop, computer facilities, technical support, library and friends to chat to and bounce ideas off, all under one roof, then suddenly it was gone!

I think for me it was really important to get a studio space and maintain the momentum I had towards the end of my time at college, but I also think it can be important for some people to reflect on where their work is going or whether they want to keep making work at all. I got a studio space, a part-time job and kept making work as and when I could. I had sold some work from my degree show and made some good contacts and received one or two invitations to show in exhibitions. I also began to organize one or two shows with friends, which is a great way to keep seeing your work in gallery spaces. I certainly think it is

key not to allow yourself to become stagnant by letting work sit in the studio doing nothing. Get it out there and see what people think ... see what *you* think seeing it in a different context. Get friends round to look at your work in the studio and give feedback. It might not always be what you want to hear but it will be helpful and keeps you moving forward.

I also think that it is important to assess what your priorities are. It will not always be easy to make work; sometimes it can be difficult fitting it in with other commitments and there will be times when you might lack confidence in your work. Pray about your situation but don't worry about it. Seek God's peace first and foremost: that is what matters. I think it is important to have a perspective on your work that allows you to be making work and enjoying that process. It will not always feel easy—it will be difficult at times, but aim to make the work you were made to make, if that makes sense—get excited about it!

The art world can be quite fickle and it is important to be able to be thick-skinned sometimes. You will never please everyone; listen to advice but weigh it and consider whether you agree: it will not always be right!

Likewise, you might find that you show work in one place and it gets a cool reception, but in another place people love it—again, a reason to be showing your work lots and getting it known in the right places. Go and see lots of exhibitions too and get a feel for where you would like to exhibit your stuff.

It is worth applying for funding or opportunities—even if you don't get it, it is worth gathering your thoughts together, and writing the proposal can prove helpful when you go back into the studio.

What else ... don't be afraid of making mistakes. Everyone does it; you would be weird if you didn't get it wrong sometimes. Learn to reflect on what happened and move on. It sounds like something from a self-help book, but it's true! Anyway, a bit of serendipity is good—those mistakes often work out better than your original intention!

Lastly, I would just say that if you would like to do a postgraduate course, don't rush into it just because you're not sure what else to do; sometimes it can be good to have a bit of time out. You'll have more experience and often be able to get more out of the course that way.

16. JAMES CARY

On making opportunities in the media, defining success, and why Christians don't laugh

James Cary is a sitcom writer, mainly for BBC TV (*Miranda, My Family*) and BBC Radio (*Hut 33, Think the Unthinkable, Another Case of Milton Jones*). He has been nominated for BAFTA, RTS, Sony and Perrier awards. He lives in Fulham with his wife and two daughters, and is the elder of a church, where he preaches occasionally.

This interview was conducted as an email exchange.

AG: Maybe we could start by talking about your college experience. Was there much help for you at that time? How did you start to put together a Christian framework for what you do?

JC: That depends what you mean by 'college'. I wrote my first sketch at school when I was about twelve. In fact, my class put on a revue, parodying the teachers and school stuff. It went down very well so I was hooked on the comedy drug and the sound of laughter from an early age. Then there were more opportunities at my senior school— but it was a very Christian school, and therefore everything was rather safe and staid. This was a good and a bad thing. Good, because it forced you to think more creatively to get laughs, rather than rely on shock. It was bad, because, overall, one could feel stultified at times. But not often. I wouldn't change my schooling for anything since many Christian teachers were truly inspirational and taught me the gospel and showed me what a wonderful saviour the Lord Jesus Christ is.

It put me in good stead for university, in Durham; there was much more freedom creatively and much less accountability in a Christian context. I was a regular at the Christian Union and at church, but was soon doing comedy shows, revues and public speaking (the latter being a posh form of stand-up comedy). I was part of the Christian crowd, and the comedy crowd—but the only member of both. I suppose I could have felt isolated by this, but I think I actually found it invigorating. This is probably because I had such a good Christian foundation because of my schooling, and also I saw it as an opportunity to reach non-Christians with the gospel. At various points, I felt pressure (mainly from myself) to put positive Christian messages in secular comedy sketches, which I did from time to time, and still do, but it took me a while to work out when it was suitable and appropriate and when it wasn't.

I didn't realize it at the time, but writing comedy would be my career and I'd be dealing with these issues all day, every day, and here I am nearly fifteen years on still wrestling with the issues. In terms of putting together a Christian framework for my work, I've always been confident that comedy and Christianity fit together well, and any apparent mismatch must be theological error and not the Creator's design. The question comes down to whether we believe that Christ laughed. The gospels never show him laughing, and yet he drew people to himself, told stories and shocked the crowds with satire, sarcasm and even impersonating Pharisees. Christ was a comedian. Clearly he was, and is, plenty of other things too,

but I've always been confident that Christians can laugh, should laugh and probably don't laugh enough. And, therefore, I've never been too disheartened about finding a way through.

AG: I remember you quoting Jesus at some event last year, I think, saying, 'he who has ears to hear, let him hear', and the play on words for ears of corn and ears to hear. It got me thinking how comedy can be culturally bound. Do you think there's humour in the Bible that we just don't see/get because we're years apart from the original writers and jokes get lost in translation? Or are there other reasons we don't laugh as much as we could?

JC: There's loads of comedy in the Bible. Much of it hasn't survived either translation or decent preaching. It can feel a bit like learning Shakespeare at school, where the teacher has to tell you where the jokes are. I really think the comedy in passages should be heightened more, since the incongruity is often staggering and the people at the time and the writer of the book of the Bible were, I'm sure, amused by what happened. We've rather forgotten how amazing—and funny—it is that Jesus could raise people from the dead. And yet he can and he does. Imagine the awkwardness of standing near Jesus when he calls Lazarus out of the tomb, wondering what's going to happen next. It is a scene ripe with comedy. There is a very funny scene in John's gospel with the man born blind, and lots of to-ing and fro-ing like a French farce, where the Pharisees are intently questioning the man, until he says, 'Hey, you seem very interested in this Jesus bloke. Oh! I get it! You want to become his followers too!' at which point they go berserk. Jesus riding into Jerusalem on a donkey is funny. Jesus being the incarnate God is so bizarre as to be comically surprising. Jesus becoming incarnate and being tried and sentenced to death and mocked and crucified is the darkest of dark comedy—not least because it has a most wonderful punchline.

AG: It strikes me, as Christians we should really be able to laugh the most because we're free to live by grace. Since we take the gospel seriously we don't have to be so serious about ourselves. Or is that too simplistic?

JC: This whole area is a minefield. In one sense, Christians are right to be cautious for a number of good reasons. Offending God

is undoubtedly a foolish and blasphemous thing to do. Proverbs warns against foolishness—and mockery, against becoming a person who heaps scorn and derision on everything. Also, comedy can offend others, which is not something we should go out of our way to do. But all of the above can make Christians bland and, ludicrously, joyless. We need to look at Jesus again. He wasn't just great company, but outrageously satirical. Now, Jesus had perfect knowledge of all things, so we need to be cautious about taking his way of talking as a licence for ourselves, but he spoke the truth. Sometimes, Christians need to be offended because they themselves are offensive to God, for their lovelessness, lack of joy or selfishness. The church is not exempt from criticism—but to speak the truth plainly, humorously and in the right way takes skill, practice and a thick skin. All of that said, my comedy isn't primarily satirical or cleverly mocking unbelief, but stories, characters and situations.

AG: You've organized events for Christians working professionally in the arts through Blueprint and also been involved with after-hours stuff at festivals like Greenbelt and New Word Alive. What do you hear as the main issues affecting Christians in the arts and media today? Where are the opportunities? What are the challenges?

JC: This is a tough one—because everyone's different and faces different struggles. Plus there are others who are more directly involved in pastoring in this area who'd be more qualified to speak on this subject, but I could offer a few thoughts here, and one in particular. The basic problem is often that people don't connect their Christian life with their work life. The two seem so distant that they never meet or interact, and this can lead to a number of dysfunctions. One is disenchantment with church. Creatives often feel isolated anyway, especially as they are types who see themselves as commentators on society, but if one keeps one's work separate, and one doesn't allow the fellowship of the church and the preaching of God's word to bear on that work, soon one will feel like one is living in two worlds, and not in a good way. Sometimes people drift away from good Bible-teaching churches into loose federations of Christian creatives and much spiritual discontentment ensues, or worse—contentment with false teaching. This is partly a failure of church, and of pastoring and preaching. But it is often a self-

inflicted wound and might be one that sometimes never heals.

Another side effect of keeping work and church separate is that work becomes more frustrating because it doesn't seem to be going anywhere. It seems pointless or, worse, vain. Again, this is often a failure of church which views media, arts and culture with suspicion (sometimes rightly so), but if you don't know why you're working, you'll soon find the going tough. Lots of Christians have spiritual crises because they don't have the right biblical expectations for their work, and what it is for and how they fit into God's plan for the redemption of the world. What Blueprint is seeking to do—along with a number of initiatives by other groups—is get ourselves familiar with the Bible, and work out how God sees work, how he sees our creative art, and how we can do it better for his glory and purposes. It's great to pray, network and encourage each other—and plenty of networks are strong on all of those—but there is no substitute for working out a biblical vocation. Protestants used to be big on this, but, like many things, it seems to have fallen away. In order to get some vocation, and decent teaching on creative arts and work, I did a lot of reading, listening and consulting.

It was worth spending the time since work was what I planned spending 40 hours a week doing for 48 weeks of the year for the next 50 years. In a way, I'm surprised more people don't try and work out the point of what they're doing in their work life. Anyway, during this time I considered full-time Christian ministry, but rejected it when I realized that I was passionate about comedy and storytelling—and was gifted at writing dialogue and plotting sitcom episodes. It's now the thing that makes me leap out of bed with joy because I believe I'm doing what God made me do. This is the point to quote Eric Liddell's oft-quoted but barely heeded line, 'I believe God made me for a purpose, but he also made me fast. And when I run I feel His pleasure.' The challenge, then, is to get a biblical mandate for your work, so that when you work, and excel in your field, you feel God's pleasure. If you've got a Bible, the mandate is sitting in your hand. You'll just need to read a bit more closely.

AG: You mentioned this was something the Protestants used to be big on. Can you elaborate on that? Why do you think we have lost this sense of working out good theology in the workplace? I see it in a few guys like Sparks and even the folks up at the Leith School of Art but you don't hear it preached regularly from the pulpit.

JC: Protestantism is tricky to define, not least because it defines itself by what it is not—Catholicism. That was the original 'Protest' of Protestantism. And yet many of the great novelists, film-makers, painters and writers of the last five hundred years have been Catholics. G. K. Chesterton is frequently quoted by evangelicals, and yet he converted to Roman Catholicism. Dorothy L. Sayers was another great writer and thinker—again, Catholic. J. R. R. Tolkien too. Can one think of a famously Protestant author, architect or artisan? C. S. Lewis was an Anglican but was no evangelical. It's worth asking the question, 'What are evangelicals frightened of?'

I think the answer to that question could be 'frivolity'. Artists, writers, designers and film-makers are frequently deemed to be at best surplus to requirements, and at worst an unholy distraction. But a distraction from what? Evangelism. As Christendom has crumbled and active Christian faith declined in the West, the greatest need is deemed to be evangelism. This is something the Catholics have traditionally been less bothered about since their ecclesiology is brimming with self-confidence. Protestants, however, like to talk about the Great Commission to make disciples of all nations. This commission is often preached as The Great Commandment, often to the exclusion of all others. The Christian life ceases to be about life, family, work, relationship and community, but winning arguments, gaining converts and expanding the church. The Great Commission is, of course, to be obeyed with joy and relish. To proclaim Christ and his gospel is a privilege and an honour. But when evangelism becomes not just 'the thing to do', but 'the only thing to do', we are in danger of making an emphasis that the Bible does not make. The Great Commission does not and should not trump all cultural activity. But the moment it does, everything the Christian does is weighed and evaluated for its evangelistic usefulness. And therefore any art or media that is not evangelistically explicit can be construed as a waste of time and/ or resources, or considered to be a missed opportunity. We functionally become Gnostics, suspicious of the physical and the sensual.

How can this misplaced emphasis work out in real life? It means that when considering what job to take, one considers whether the workplace in question is a good one to evangelize. Will I be able to have Christian conversations? Will I be able to start a Bible study or a Christian Union? Will this job pay well so I can give lots of money to the evangelistic work my church is doing? Will it pay well so I can provide for my family? Is this workplace near my church so I can invite my colleagues along to events and services? These are all useful questions to ask, but they omit some serious key ones. Consider this: you're going to spend 40 hours a week (at least) working in this place doing a job. Have you considered whether the job is useful? Does it benefit others (beyond your own salary)? Is it an honest profession? Do you have the skills for it? Do you feel called to this line of work? Will it satisfy you, given that you have been made by God to work? Given the new earth will be a renewed old earth, how will your work under God contribute to that?

These questions are universal and don't just apply to creative Christians. But doctors and teachers do jobs that seem immediately useful and therefore in no need of justification. Actors, journalists and cameramen have a harder time. What this latter group need to remember is that in the new earth, the doctors will need to retrain since there'll be no more sickness, and the teachers too, since there'll be no children. The full-time evangelists will have no one to evangelize. The artists, however, will continue to make culture in a real and physical way for an eternity. So we're getting a head start on that.

Ultimately, we need to ask ourselves what we're Christians for. And if we're evangelizing others, what sort of life are we offering? Again, if we only evangelize, and offer a life of evangelism, what we're offering is a huge spiritual pyramid scheme, where the only aim is to sign up more people. No, the Christian life is to be lived to the full. And when we boldly proclaim Christ, and seek to persuade others to come to know him, we should be offering life to the full: not a bland, colourless, culturally emaciated existence that is doctrinally correct but lacking any sign of joy or laughter. The world has a happy ending. Christ returns and makes all things new. But to spend time with a lot of evangelical Christians, you would struggle to find that out.

AG: It might be easier to quantify 'success' in evangelism because you can see when people become Christians. Harder, though, to see when you're doing things well as an actor, writer or painter. Do you base success on the critics' review, audience response or number of awards on the mantelpiece?

JC: It's a good question for artists in general: How do I know if I'm doing well? Am I impressing people with my work? If so, which people—the audience or industry peers? The comedy industry is still very snobby about mainstream success. Loads of comedians can't bear Michael McIntyre and give many reasons why he isn't funny, failing to realize that Michael McIntrye regularly delights crowds of several thousand people at a time. It's a mixture of jealousy, resentment and frustration that the mainstream audience seems content with the obvious rather the nuanced. It's like that in every industry, I'm sure. Does one 'sell out' and go for the mainstream and take the money? Or does one 'stay true' and keep the respect of one's peers (the comedian Stewart Lee firmly remains in this latter camp)? It's the constant dilemma that the creative finds him- or herself in.

The creative Christian, however, is liberated from this conundrum—or at least is in theory. The question that any Christian needs to ask him- or herself is how he or she brings glory to Christ—in all things. This includes work—not just the content but the method. A Christian musician could bring glory to God by being hailed as a genius and awarded the Mercury Music Prize or a Grammy. But if they achieve this artistic and/or commercial success at the expense of their character, leaving behind failed marriages or neglected children, they are not honouring Christ at all and their work is nothing by a clanging gong. We all know where we ourselves are most likely to fail in this regard—and fail we surely will at times. It's a good thing to pursue professional excellence, but it can come at a price. Recently, I saw a documentary about the mania that some chefs experience as they seek the validation of Michelin stars, leading, in some cases, to breakdown and even suicide. This is clearly a godless way of approaching one's work. Work is important and something we were all made by God to do. But it is not everything. It's made by God, and should never become a god.

And let us return to your original question. Success in evangelism is not always obvious. True success in this area is preaching the gospel faithfully, winsomely and comprehensibly—in word and deed.

It is the work of God's Holy Spirit to honour that by opening blind eyes to the glory of Christ. You can preach as well as Tim Keller, but if God chooses not to illuminate hearts by his Spirit, people won't become Christians. In the same way, one can pursue a career in art, comedy, journalism or circus skills, and you may be doing your work brilliantly—but it is God who grants success, not a panel of judges, a TV commissioner, a critic or even an audience. We should remember that every aspect of our lives is in his hands.

The Bible regularly uses the phrases 'But as for me' or 'but as for you', encouraging God's people not to worry about the success of others, or the esteem of the world. We should seek a quiet life, and work with our hands in humble obedience. If God gives us an Oscar or a yacht for that work, or a lifetime of contented obscurity, that's up to him. He is good— and remains so regardless of the content of our trophy cabinet or bank account.

AG: This is such a big question for all of us who are Christians and working in the arts. How else do you measure if you're doing things well? How do you think God defines success?

JC: There is a wonderful hymn that begins one verse with the line 'Riches I heed not, nor man's empty praise'. It's a great thing to sing, although the brevity and poetry hide a multitude of ambiguities. Should we really not heed wealth or the praise of men? Do these things really mean nothing to us? 'How do I know when I'm doing well?'

Of course, some say that they perform for an audience of one— being God, obviously. That's true, and sounds great and godly. Well done. But God has given us all responsibilities, and our craft does not take place in a vacuum. God has given us a vocation and a desire to please him, and please him we must. But he has also given some of us spouses and children to provide for. Therefore, the work we do must not only be pleasing in God's sight, but commercially viable, lest our pursuit of excellence becomes a selfish vanity that causes hardship for others. We are not to be a burden to others but to work with our hands, making enough to be hospitable and generous.

We need to be mindful of our age and stage. When I was a young single man, clearly I had more creative freedom and was able to live on very little, having just been a student. Now I have to pay rent for a three-bedroom house in London, and look after a wife, two children and a Ford Mondeo (no kidding). To piously assert that I am only interested in God's opinion of my work is a little disingenuous. Life is complicated— and that doesn't have to be a cop-out to pursue wealth.

We can easily fall into the very British trap of assuming that all wealth is suspect and must have been acquired at some cost to someone somewhere. Either someone has been exploited or artistic values have been compromised and the artist in question has 'sold out'. But this misrepresents how wealth is portrayed in the Bible. Wealth is not suspect, but a blessing (e.g. to Job or Abraham). It is also a responsibility and a possible snare (e.g. to the Rich Young Ruler). We must live open-handedly, but for those of us who are full-time creatives, our God-given crafts and skills must be put to use, and our God-given families must be supported. It is normal for these two to be linked, and therefore 'riches' need to be 'heeded' at some point.

But what about 'man's empty praise'? Recently, a sitcom I co-wrote was nominated for an RTS Writing Award and a BAFTA. Is this empty? Clearly, many of us value the opinion of our peers very highly, but this is partly because we know that our peers understand how hard our craft is. Their opinion does matter. Should we pursue their approval at all costs? Of course not. And this is easier said than done. But to be praised by men for work done is a good thing, as long as it is not the thing that gets us out of bed.

The main problem is that we compartmentalize and divide our lives into chunks and sections and set one off against the other. Our desires to create good work are given by God, as are our families, peers, money and awards. God is in control and it is he that decides who wins the Pulitzer and the Nobel Prize for Literature. So don't worry. Get your head down and work, as if to the Lord.

One last thing. I recently ran a session on this idea at my church weekend away, and in groups we thought about how we define success. One lady came up with a great aspiration: to create work that lasts. A great example of this would be Tolkien's *Lord of the Rings,* which is improving with age. This is a noble thing to aim for—although not the only thing. Sometimes artists are brilliant at catching a moment with a picture, a photograph or a comedy character (e.g. Harry Enfield's Loadsamoney). But again, if we lock ourselves away to pursue timeless perfection because we seek validation by critics not yet born, we will run into danger. Like many things in life, it's a balancing act. But we must remember to hold all things in open, grateful hands because it is all a gift from God. The moment we tighten a fist around one of those things, we begin to harm ourselves and those we love. That, surely, is failure?

Comedians—ask yourself, which of the Goons would you most like to be? Milligan, who pursued comedy to the point of madness? Sellers, who was haunted by all kinds of demons? Or Secombe—the magnanimous gentleman who was ultimately more of a man than most of us?

AG: What advice would you give to other writers trying to get started in the industry?

JC: To people trying to get into the media in general, I'd seriously advise work experience. I only realized that I wanted to be a writer by doing work experience with BBC News and with a magazine—and realized I really didn't enjoy that. I was a runner on a TV comedy show called *The Friday Night Armistice,* and realized that I didn't enjoy TV production either, and recognized that I was only really interested in writing. So, write to people who do what you want to do and ask if you can hang out with them. The more specific the better. Spell their name right. Be polite. Make it easy for them to do you a favour.

If you think that you could be a writer, the best thing to do is write. Write a script, or a short story or a novel. Write something you'd actually like to read, or a TV show you would want to watch. There is no substitute for passion and enjoyment when it comes to writing. Then write it. All of it. Finish it. Put it to one side—and then come back to it. Rewrite it. Then edit it. Then edit it properly, getting rid of anything that isn't brilliant. Then send it to people who might 'get it'. You're better sending it to strangers who might 'get it' than friends who probably won't. The strangers who read it and respond will be far more honest and useful than the friend who still wants to be your friend afterwards. The chances are that nothing will happen with that thing you've written. It's only really a calling card, but it's a start, a statement of intent, a confidence booster and something to talk about.

For comedy writing, it is well worth just putting something on and having your work performed. I'd avoid doing it at your church because it'll be a weird audience (that's a topic for another time). Go to a local fringe theatre or pub. If you can get to the Edinburgh Fringe, even better. Put something on there. It'll probably vanish without trace, but you will find like-minded comedians and friends who may end up being friends and colleagues for many years to come.

BBC Online has a useful resource called Writersroom, which is worth checking regularly. Read, read, read. Read novels, stories, screenplays as well as one or two books about writing. Here's a less obvious one: Learn to use a word processor properly so your scripts are well presented and legible. Sometimes I edit scripts for the BBC and I'm astonished at how clueless some writers are at the basic craft of word processing, and it doesn't make me all that keen to work with them again, since I have to unpick all of their dreadful formatting.

After a few years, you might be getting nowhere, and have received little, if any, encouragement. That's the time to think about doing something else. You're still in God's image, and your mum still loves you. You're just not a writer. And that may turn out to be a wonderful blessing!

17. KIERAN DODDS

On what makes a good picture, shooting bats and how faith informs photography

Kieran Dodds was the UK and
Ireland Picture Editors' Young
Photographer of the Year in 2005
and went on to win a whole host of
awards including 1st Prizes in World
Press Photo (2006), the Scottish
Press Photo Awards (2007) and
The UK Press Photographer's Year
(2010).

His publications portfolio includes
the *New York Times, The Sunday
Times Magazine* (London), Canon
Europa, Homecoming 2009
(Scottish Government), GEO
(France, Germany & Russia),
National Geographic, Shell and
Tearfund UK. Kieran lives and
works in Glasgow.

AG: Your route into photography
was far from conventional. How did
you get into the industry?

KD: I began taking pictures at a
young age and remember taking a
shot of a raccoon in Canada aged
eight. The shot was so good I had
to tell my dad. I haven't changed
that much in 20 years; that's now
my work: taking interesting things
and telling others about them. I
wanted to be a journalist at school
because I enjoyed writing, but
careers advice didn't extend that far
and the computer told me to be a
biology teacher. I wanted to study
zoology at university to help me
become a wildlife film-maker (*à la*
Attenborough) but also loved the

origins of life and evolution and so embarked on four years at Aberdeen.

I documented student life, night safaris in the cold north, and spent more on processing and film than beer, which isn't hard at £1 a pint. I loved people's reaction to the shots and it spurred me on to keep shooting. By third year I was planning an expedition to Malawi with a friend to study blue monkeys for our dissertation and it was on that trip two key things changed.

Firstly, I spent more time trying to photograph the animals and the dramatic mountain plateau we were living on than I spent recording their behaviour. They just sat, ate and slept; it wasn't dissimilar to my last three years. By the end of the trip I had shot nearly 2000 frames (on film), which was a vast collection. Flying over the massif on the last week I thought, 'This is the kind of job I like; I'm going to be a photographer.' I never published the work but did, years later, show editors at *National Geographic,* who praised it.

Secondly, while there I was experiencing a personal crisis. Nothing visible, just a constant doubt intellectually and emotionally inside that something was not

right. I had been wrestling with the veracity of the Bible and in particular the physical resurrection of Jesus and the origins of life. I had worked out that I had to decide one way or other before I came back from Africa. On the mountain in Malawi I was struck by the lack of meaning and purpose in life if it was all just a process. My scientific worldview had been seriously undermined by my investigations and the facts would not fit—Jesus had risen from the dead—but I was desperate to find a scientific explanation. I put off the inevitable until I returned to Scotland.

In my honours year, while editing the student paper and writing my dissertation, I read a Billy Graham book, *How to Be Born Again.* It made sense of the moral dimension to my struggle; the facts and the feelings connected in a way I had never understood and I prayed that Christ would be my shepherd and lead me forward. This had profound impact on my direction and choices in life.

By now, I was thinking how to spend the rest of my life. With the knowledge that God loved me, I reasoned that he had made me for a purpose and it was to enjoy him. It was naïve but not untrue, though untangling my will from 'thy will' is a constant challenge. So with this purpose in mind, I embarked on a career in journalism which I had also fallen in love with. My first work experience was at the *Press and Journal* newspaper in Aberdeen. We covered local news at primary schools, cow auctions and everything you'd expect from the north-east but I was properly hooked when the photographer was given a box of langoustine while doing a business job at a fish factory!

By the end of my university course, I had undertaken some freelance work for them at Highland games and graduations (including my own). I left Aberdeen and worked as a writer for a Scottish Sunday paper at the Edinburgh Festival before being 'called' back to Aberdeen for a news agency. The *P&J* had been contacted by the agency asking if anyone would be suitable. I was the only person who was keen, they were told. And so it began …

AG: You've worked on projects as diverse as photographing bats in Africa to drug addicts in Scotland. Are there overarching themes that interest you as a photographer— that inform your work—or is it just a case of doing whatever seems to be good for next?

KD: I was trained as a press photographer, which means I was directed to stories, for the most part, by my commissioning editors. Over time I have developed my own work as well. If someone is paying you to shoot Fort William Football Club you will shoot Fort William Football Club. That's partly why I love press work: its diversity has opened my eyes to the world and directed me to things I would not have discovered otherwise—life in its fulness, bad and good.

From my early days, nature and creation have loomed large in my work and I pursue this where possible to balance the more prevalent theme in media: the fall. I shot the bats to point people to the order and beauty of creation, to remind us there is purpose and meaning beyond our own personal delusions and despair. I won a bursary to shoot anything I wanted and thought I should do something to document and alleviate suffering, which is very popular in photojournalism, but this story appeared and I thought it needed to be told and it was too interesting.

Eight million bats in a forest! They are unpopular creatures yet God made them so there must be beauty there. I challenged myself and came out better for it.

Due to time and finance I have done more human-interest work in recent years. Heroin addiction is an old story, but although there is nothing new under the sun, I was nervous about being a cliché. I see so much hopelessness in work on addiction, it shocks but leaves the audience unsure what to do except turn away shaking their heads (or nodding at the gruesome aesthetic). This story was about people getting clean and becoming whole again, so it had a positive direction even if it was still very dark in content.

With the decline in editorial I am now seeking funding for my own work, which is exciting, but sometimes I would just love someone calling up and saying, 'Hey, Kieran, can you go and shoot some portraits of chefs on the Isle of Skye?'—I love doing commissions. Doing my own work involves more time in the office and less on the road. At the end of the day, I am a professional and someone has to pay the bills, but commissions free me to explore new ideas and communicate what I find, which is why I like this business.

AG: I take your point about avoiding clichés, which is tricky when we live in an age when everybody owns a camera. What makes an image stand out for you?

KD: Martin Parr said, 'It's the most democratic art form, but it's painfully difficult to be good at it.' And his work stands out to me, not because it's bright and recognizable, but because he focuses right in on things that interest him, often mundane, overlooked details. I think this jumps out of the photographer's world: the curiosity of the observer. If we are just framing things nicely it lacks that zing. Composition and technical skill are vital but the photographer must be willing and able to convey meaning. Documentary or photojournalism can sound like a dry and clinical recording of what's in front but it's like good preaching: it's 'logic on fire', as Lloyd-Jones would say, the rational with the visceral, the brain and the bowels. I am more forgiving of bad technical work if the image captured is arresting emotionally.

AG: This whole rational with the visceral thing ('brain and the bowels'—I like it) is a fascinating issue. I think we see it a bit in Genesis when God says the trees are pleasing to the sight *and* good for food. Psalmist David writes that the visual attributes of the creation serve as one great signpost to the unseen characteristics of God (Psalm 19, I think). How can the Christian worldview be worked out in photos? It seems a little trite to say, 'Right, I'm going to take a photo about atonement today', so how do you begin to approach issues of faith in a visual medium? ... Or do you even have to? Also, the creation is full of stuff that doesn't 'say' anything more profound than 'Isn't blue nice!'

KD: I suppose, how do we approach issues of faith in life in general? I suppose I start by seeking first the Kingdom in my personal life, intentionally turning to the Lord in wonder, love and praise. By saturating my mind, it filters into my behaviour and feelings, which will then leak out into my work. In a sense everything I do should be touched by this outpouring of faith. This will affect the subjects I choose to cover, or the way in which I cover them. So the bats were to show beauty, the addicts to convey hope and dignity to the 'worst' of society and the Zimbabwean essays to communicate compassion to those who are hurting.

Obviously I have to shoot what's there and not shoehorn my worldview onto something, and it's not always as obvious. How do you shoot a phone-mast protest? With righteous anger? Can people discern a difference between my work and a non-Christian's? I don't know but I cannot detach the way I shoot from my worldview as much as the next man and will seek to explain this at lectures or chatting with viewers. The creation displays God's eternal power and divine nature, which we all know but each of us suppresses this knowledge. In my work I want people to take a moment to 'consider the birds' and trust the Spirit to use this in softening hearts to the gospel. Pictures are a blunt tool to articulate the gospel but even a blunt sledgehammer has power.

18. INTERFACE ARTS RELAY GROUP

On living for Christ at art college, surviving your final year show and beyond

The Relay programme is a year of discipleship and training run by the Universities and Colleges Christian Fellowship. In return, Relay workers help UCCF staff workers and students in the Christian Unions. In 2010, twelve arts Relay workers met regularly through the year to critique one another's work, pray, study the Bible and help each other make good work.

This interview was recorded after dinner at their final meeting.

Part one: Introductions

AG: So this book's about trying to break down some of the issues we face as artists and as Christians— what to do when you graduate, how to pay the bills, how to budget, as well as some of the biblical stuff that we've looked at over the year. It's designed to be a bumper book for Christians working in the arts, with practical stuff as well as the theory. And this section in the book is interviewing artists who are Christians and asking them about their experiences and trying to join up the theory with the practice … so let's have a chat for about twenty minutes about life as art students, being at art college and how you do that as a Christian. Why don't we start by going round the group and saying who we are and what we do.

Ashleigh Breda: My name is Ashleigh Breda and I am a fine artist.

Dan Curtis: You are indeed, Madam.

Rupert Empleton-Smith: My name's Rupert and I play and write songs.

Daniel Bate: I'm Dan and I'm a graphic designer.

Matthew Weston: I'm Matthew and I'm a musician and a poet.

David Latcham: I'm Dave Latcham and I'm a graphic designer.

Lois Adams: I'm Lois Adams and I'm a set designer.

Lizzie Kevan: I'm Lizzie. Yep, I'm an illustrator.

Lucinda Metcalfe: I'm Luci and I'm currently a painter.

Rael Mason: I'm Rael and I do poetry.

Dan Curtis: I'm Dan and I do sculpture and a bit of stand-up comedy.

Holly Reger: I'm Holly and I'm doing creative writing.

Millie Styles: I'm Millie and I'm an actor.

AG: And I'm Ally and I'm a painter.

Part two: How was art college for you?

AG: Right then, first, what was life like for you guys at college? What was your experience as Christians at art college? And how did your expectations of art college live up to your experiences?

DB: I think it was only later on at college that people realized that I was a Christian, so I think I missed quite a few opportunities to start with.

AG: When have been significant times for you? When have you grown?

DB: Probably at university getting stuck into CU and doing a year on the executive committee—really quite a tough year in terms of balancing time, work and CU.

AG: Were there many Christians around who helped you with the design side of things?

DB: Not really, to be honest. There weren't many Christians that I knew of and not much Christian support in terms of art and design. Which, really, I think I could have done with because I'd quite like to go back now and redo some of my work and approach it from a Christian point of view or think about how I can do it in a way that gives glory to God.

LA: For me, I came from a really small village in Wales with a strong sense of community and at the thought of going to London I feared it was going to be really tough, competitive and hard. But there was such a creative atmosphere. It was buzzing, and there was a real

community and it was not what I had feared.

AG: Did anyone else have a really positive experience like that?

DC: Yeah, when I started at college it was just after I had become a Christian. So at first it was a time of real refining, I guess, a time of being broken a lot. My thinking was starting to change, and some ideas were becoming stronger. Growing in knowing God, with little Christian support at first, changed my outlook and what I was doing in the studio.

AG: How did you see your work starting to change?

DC: I thought, what am I really doing? Is it all right for me to be doing this? Is this what God really wants me to do? And then I came across people like yourself, Ally, and other people in the arts and started to pray with one older Christian on my course who found out that I was a Christian, and that was really amazing and helped a lot. As to the work itself, I guess as I changed, as my heart was changed by the Holy Spirit, it affected the ideas shaping my work. My concerns—with material combinations and material relationships—are still very much the same, but my convictions have become stronger.

AB: It came out quite early on at college that I was a Christian. And there was an acceptance of it all round my course, which was really amazing. At first people were quite afraid to come to me because we had a lot of people on my course who had ideas about what Christians believe that weren't necessarily true, about homosexuality, for example. But my tutors knew where I stood. I always saw redemptive themes coming through in my work, like 'resurrection' and 'breathing life into materials', which I think most of my tutors accepted. I was lucky that one of my tutors happened to be a vicar. So in that sense I think they were supportive of my work, but it felt like I could never say God's name out loud, like it wasn't allowed. It was OK to have an idea of a force or something else, but never to express anything specific about Jesus Christ.

AG: One of the things that James Elkins says in that book *On the Strange Place of Religion in Contemporary Art* is that you can talk about issues of faith if you're being ironic or cynical but if you have sincere faith in God or sincere religious belief, then this is a problem.

AB: Yes. It was like that.

AG: Did anyone else have an experience like that?

MW: I guess a little bit. I did quite an academic music degree and I guess you look at the last four hundred years and the huge influence of the church. But then there's a sense that it's part of our general music tradition. So we appreciate singing the hymns and the mass, but the words might as well be gibberish symbols. People are surprised if you think they mean something. 'Oh, you take it seriously today?' 'Oh, you're writing a piece of religious music?' 'Why would you want to do that?'

HR: I had almost the opposite experience in my theatre degree. From the very first day I had the opportunity to tell people I was a Christian, and I think I was the only Christian in my year, so word spread like wildfire. But as a result, I wasn't asked to take on any serious roles and my opinion wasn't really taken that seriously, especially in my first year until, by default, because I was in a line-up, it was decided that I would play a rape victim in a piece of physical theatre. It was only at that point, when I said I'd do it, that everybody's jaws dropped and they thought, oh, I didn't think she would do that or could do that, and it was after that when people started asking me my opinion on their performance and asked me to be in their group, which was nice. But sadly it showed how fickle the situation was, and I know that my being a Christian had limited the opportunities for me to be involved.

AG: Did you have experiences like that at acting school as well, Millie?

MS: Yeah, I think with it being a really secular environment, any talking about Jesus was just laughed away, so I would get mocked in essays if I talked about my faith and what I believed. In class and in the studio there were just constant ridiculing of religion, and I found it hard that the lecturers and the tutors in their position of authority were having these opinions and being quite open about them, and that everybody then assumed what they said was true—how to speak into

that and be a Christian? It wasn't straightforward.

RES: I think that's one side of the coin. But I have an actor friend at church who has opportunities to pray with people, you know, before they go on stage. So there is that other side too.

HR: I think it differs from one person to another. With my friends on my course there was a difference between what they thought and the views of the university body. In conversations outside the studio I could talk about faith, but I couldn't take that into the studio.

Part three: What was it like being a Christian and an art student?

AG: I wonder if this is something that's quite specific to the performing arts. As a painter I make this thing in isolation then put it up on the wall for others to see, so I make work more or less on my own. But when you work in theatre or in the recording studio you're working more in collaboration. You're depending more on the opinions of others. Does that mean other people's opinions affect you more, perhaps?

DL: Yeah, because in terms of graphic design, I don't think this issue really came up that much. You're set a brief and there are limitations and restrictions and then you work from that, and so how people think about your work and their opinions of your work are sort of based on the boundaries and restrictions of the brief rather than on personal opinion. You might put your own twist on it but that's your work, whereas they'll critique it very much based on the brief itself.

AG: Did you find that the discussion of being a Christian and a designer came up much on your design courses?

DL: I think more just in personal relationships rather than in the work itself … it affected how people related around me. In a positive way, I think. In the group I was with, people knew I was a Christian. So when someone made a really crude joke they'd end up saying, 'Oh sorry, David' or something like that. They'd apologize when they swore and stuff or stop doing that regularly.

LK: For me issues of faith never came up, really, until I was asked to design a book on voodoo. It was supposed to be an image for my portfolio and I didn't want that image to represent what I did, so I asked if I could change the brief and the tutor was fine. That's OK. It wasn't really a problem. The only time that faith really came up was in one-to-one conversations in the studio. And with one guy once I said I was off to the Christian Union that night and he said, 'Oh, so that's why you work so hard!'

Part four: How did you manage your time?

AG: I think one of the big issues is, how do you manage your time between all the various parts of your life—between the coursework, CU, church, mates—especially when you're in your final year or you're involved with leading CU. How did you guys handle that?

DC: I'll tell you how I didn't handle it. In my second year I guess I didn't grasp grace, really. As quite a young

Christian I thought God wanted me to do everything so, yeah, I ended up being in the Christian Union, being on the leadership team of Christian Union, organizing a Bible study at my house, getting involved with an International Café and then another International Café on a Friday night. And because of all that my artwork went downhill. For one project I did a final piece, and then four months after that I just did the same piece again because I hadn't made anything else. And it was a bit embarrassing, I guess, because one of my tutors asked, 'So are you going to do the same thing again for the next show?' And it was when Peter Smith—the guy who does the etching, yeah?—it was when he said at an Interface Arts meeting that 1 per cent read the Bible, the other 99 per cent read the Christian; that if other artists are seeing you and going, 'If that's what Christians are like—come in half the time, half-arsed, do half the work and don't really care about their art—then I don't really want to become a Christian if that's what being a Christian involves.' I care about my art. I don't want to make crap art. And it was really powerful when I heard that.

LM: I think at art college for me it was kind of different. I was

slightly messed up before I became a Christian and my work was going downhill anyway. Then I became a Christian and actually took it more seriously. I don't think it was because I'd learnt anything particularly. It was just that I wasn't going out so much and I was a bit more aware of myself and having more integrity, I think. And I was really encouraged a year after I'd finished my degree when I was doing my MA and the head of painting came and visited my studio and took me out for coffee and recognized that I'd come to this secular environment and that I was a Christian, and he sort of said to me that I was one whom he thought had integrity and whose work he respected, and that the people in whom he saw something like that were all Christians.

AG: That's interesting.

DC: That's really great!

AG: Sometimes I find Christians at college who are working really hard at CU but not their course, or working really hard at their art but sort of on the fringe of CU or church or Christian things. Surely it doesn't have to be like those extremes. Surely there's a middle ground, isn't there?

DL: I think we have to take the work seriously but not turn it into an idol.

DC: Absolutely.

DL: If it's the making of the thing that rules your life, that's because you're turning it into an idol.

MW: I think that's something I was trying not to do. There were lots of people on my course and they were doing nothing but music, music, music, and they were competing against each other. I kind of hoped that my identity wasn't in those things, but what I think actually happened was that I ended up not taking my course seriously, so I didn't quite grasp the middle ground in the way that I might have done.

Part five: How did you manage the pressures of your degree show?

AG: One of the tough pressure points for me as a student was degree show time and managing time, work and sleep. I remember my aunty came over to see my final-year show and she walked right past me in the corridor because she didn't recognize me. I had to call her back and she said, 'Oh, you just look dead!' I was working way too hard and not eating and not sleeping, and sometimes there can be a lot of pressure from people who say that's the time to be the witness; that's the time to be different—and all you want to do is get this thing finished.

But maybe some of you did better than me in managing that final stage of your degree. I know many of you did. Would you have any advice for others on how to manage your time, energy and resources at that time?

HR: Realize there are actually hours in the morning before eleven o'clock. Someone said to me, 'Why don't you get up at eight and then you can start at nine.' And then I found if I do about eight or nine hours of work from nine o'clock, then actually I could have the whole rest of the evening to either rest or go to CU or see friends. And actually doing work in the day was a bit of a revelation to me in my second and third year. I think you're far more productive if you get up and just get going earlier.

MW: My problem was in not getting going early enough in the year. I thought, 'Right it's due in two months' time, that's plenty of time. I'm not going to bother doing anything today.' I had that attitude throughout my degree and then I realized in my final year that that wasn't going to work, and it was a nightmare then trying to learn how to be motivated when the deadline wasn't near.

RES: Yeah, when you get an assignment set, what's stopping you getting started straight away? Just get on with it.

AG: We were taught to imagine the deadline was a week beforehand. Perhaps I could have done with imagining it a year beforehand!

DL: God gives you three whole years at uni to steward well, and not just the last two weeks. I was rubbish at that. The five days before my final hand-in I slept for twelve hours, and then the day after my final hand-in I slept for twelve hours.

RES: And it's a really good witness, as Peter [Smith] was saying: people notice who hands in their work on time.

DC: And actually that's a real trust-builder as people see that you can handle your time and then they come to you and ask your help or ask you to be rep for the class or whatever, because you get your work in on time. That's really powerful.

AB: There's a risk, though, because as I started my first year I basically started working hard from the beginning, and I was really determined to get a first for every assignment, and I did. But then everybody else was pacing themselves and I didn't. By the time I got to the end of my first year I was losing energy. By the time I got to my third year I was the last person to get into class. I still started my days off at something like eight in the morning and I was there until eight at night. Yet I was always the last one up trying to burn a DVD for the next day or trying to finish my show work. I really got burnt out in my third year, though by God's grace I got through it.

HR: I think it's easy to forget that rest and play is part of God's design for our lives and that we need both. It's also a really good witness to your work mates: that, actually, you can take a rest and that you do know how to stop.

LM: I think CUs can be a really good witness there as a community. I remember in my final year that all the CU were there in my space helping me get it ready, and people noticed that community.

DC: Yeah, I bet!

AG: CUs can actually really help final-year students.

Part six: What advice would you give?

AG: If you could meet yourselves again at art college and you could give yourself one piece of advice, what would you say to yourself?

MW: Can I have two?

AG: You obviously needed a lot of help!

MW: Yeah, absolutely … The first is to use the opportunities of the early years well, because what I did was to waste a lot of the time when I should have listened to music, played it, read about it. I missed a lot in my first couple of years. Then in my final year I didn't have the time, so I felt like I was trying to use my third year well but couldn't because I hadn't prepared myself well enough. So make the most of *all* your time at college or uni.

The second is to get a strong grasp early on of what it means to be a Christian and a musician. I had this false idea that somehow doing lots of stuff for the CU was better than actually doing stuff for my

degree. Also, get an understanding of how to write music that reflects the knowledge that God made this world, this creation. You know, this whole creation, including music, testifies to Christ, and that's something I've only just started realizing recently; and I just wonder, if I had known all that back in my first year, how much that could have transformed the way I went about my entire degree…

DL: I'd say, spend more time with course mates. I've lost contact pretty much with everyone on my course. I built up a good network of Christian friends, which was really great in that it helped me to cope with living in London, but it meant that I neglected the more difficult thing of building up relationships with course mates, and that's rubbish because you also need a community of people who are going to be doing the same thing as you, as well as a community in which you can be a witness.

LK: I think I would have told myself to remember the gospel. I know it sounds quite simple, but quite often I got stressed out about things that didn't matter in the greater scheme of things—trying to impress everybody and look the best—I think that totally bypasses God's grace. There are great swathes of time when

I was freaking out about something or another that really wasn't relevant to life. Yeah, so remember grace.

DC: I wanted to say exactly the same, and add to that, don't be afraid to push yourself. Not in an ill [obsessive] way, but when I think about my final year—I had a studio space, access to tutors, a library, all those things—and I look back on it, I think I could have pushed myself so much harder. I could have been so much more experimental, but I was too afraid. So I'd say, don't fear: God is with you. You need to hold that line of grace.

DL: Sometimes you need to do those rubbish experiments to get onto good stuff. And don't be worried about doing those experiments.

DC: Absolutely.

DL: It's all part of the process.

AB: I would say, pace yourself, Ashleigh. And, it's OK: you don't have to work 24 hours all the time. It's OK to fail from time to time. Get more sleep and more play.

LM: I'd say definitely just try and hone some skills. Because while you're at college you've got amazing facilities and people to tell you how to use stuff. I think when I was at college I stayed clear of the print room because it wasn't my area. It felt like I had no right to go in there, but while you're a student you've got every right to go in there. Really, just be annoying to your tutors. Keep on asking them questions, because actually they'll respect you for that in the end because you've shown that you are interested. I wish I had more of that attitude: that actually I'm here right now and I've got a right to learn. Sometimes you don't feel like you do when you're in that position.

RES: I think along the same lines as Dave: I would want to talk to my course mates more and find out how they do things. And write things down, not just say, 'Oh, that's cool!' but actually write it down and take it in.

AG: Well, let's draw stumps there. Thanks, guys, that was really helpful.

19. RAEL MASON

On interdisciplinary work, writing poetry
and the dynamic between sport and art

Rael Mason studied Sports Journalism and now writes poetry for performance. He is a recent graduate.

This interview took place over tea at an arts retreat in Leeds.

AG: I think a lot of people are in the situation where they study one thing and then go on to do something completely different. You studied Sports Journalism but now you're writing poetry. So what was that transition like for you?

RM: The use of language and the power of words are part of both,

but I think I've come to see this year, particularly through what I've thought about in my art and poetry, that there's a lot more to it. I feel that I'm much stronger as a writer when I'm inspired by something. I care about sport and I wanted to communicate that in a way that helps other people to be excited about it too—and that motivation carried over into my writing this year. Yeah, the things I write poetry about aren't sporty, but they're things that I care about...

There are times I've slacked off because I've thought, 'I'll wait for the inspiration to hit me'. In one sense you can't force inspiration. But when it comes down to what I write about, it's often something external, something I've seen, that inspires me—a film that talks about love or hate or truth—that triggers my thoughts. Actually the passion was already inside me—I already cared about love; I already cared about truth, about pain, about suffering—but I needed the external trigger. Forcing myself to take the time to get away—and that might be to a pub surrounded by tons of people—that's where I've written some of my favourite stuff—it might be to my bedroom, getting alone with my thoughts. But mostly inspiration comes from writing about things that I really care about.

Coming to a greater appreciation of certain artistic disciplines also helps. I remember when Dan talked about his sculpting, about potential that he sees within the material, I thought, 'That's something that I wouldn't naturally have picked up on.' I've seen how something had affected him, that concept, that tension, when the solution doesn't seem immediately obvious, and I thought, 'That's something I'd like to write about.'

Other people's art has inspired me too, For example, how might I express what Dan expresses visually? I can go write about that. And I've found, as we've gone around galleries this year, that I've seen themes that painters have expressed that I might not be able to paint, but that I'd want to go and write some words about.

It's been a real learning curve, working with other people and finding out what they get inspired by, how they go about expressing that and then figuring how I might express it.

AG: Does working in one medium and then changing to another lead to a practice that's a jack-of-all-trades and master of none, or does working in different disciplines enrich your practice?

RM: I think I've always cared about language, but nobody had ever suggested poetry. Journalism just seemed like the obvious way to go. I thought it was something that could provide a job for me at the end and when somebody came along and said poetry could be journalism, I really connected with that.

I do think maybe we can spread ourselves too thinly. People have suggested using music with my words, that sort of thing, but I think for me, right now, the power of words absolutely fascinates me, being able to captivate people purely by what you're saying—maybe that's the skill of the words or it's the delivery or the power of what's actually being said—but I think for now I'm just trying to hold people with what I'm saying through the words. And I think for me to spread into other areas now wouldn't really be helpful. I'm sure there are people who are hugely gifted in a number of different artistic disciplines, but I think for a lot of people it wouldn't hurt their art just to focus on the particular area that they're working in.

I Met a Girl

I met a girl who reminds me I believe in love,
beyond these half hearted Valentine's measurements,
"I love you to the tune of six hundred grams of chocolate
and twelve red roses that'll be dead in a few days"
I hope that's not a metaphor,
I met a girl who reminds me I believe in love,
beyond these gift card caricatures, 'love is,
not leaving the toilet seat up'
or 'putting out the bins before you put your feet up'
or only present when things physically heat up,
I believe in love that's liable to leave your heart beat up, to a pulp,
as you daily take a gulp, of the joyous and
terrifying reality that is true love,
love not built on self preservation, or self gratification,
or anything selfish at its foundation,
other person centred love that's a reflection
of the One who created it,
but this young man's struggle, is that every time I switch on my TV,
or step out my front door, I feel like a one man army,
on the front line of a battle with a world that doesn't believe in love,
these are the days where pornography murders romance,
and if you believe in one guy, one girl, one flesh,
for life, they'll tell you no chance,
if you want to learn about chivalry, any lads' mag is a no go,
they want us hopping from bed to bed, like
we're travelling on a pogo stick,
and if I'm honest it kind of makes me sick,
because we've not liberated ourselves,
we've cheapened, abused and domesticated the
most powerful expression we ever had,
so I'll stand against the tide, look this girl straight
in the eye, and tell her everything,
when I'm with you I want to say something profound,
"my love for you is my pericardium, every
inch of my heart does it surround"

and when you smile, it makes me want to do cartwheels,
that's not just a turn of phrase, to earn your praise,
I mean I'll learn to do cartwheels just to
show you how my heart feels,
I want to grow old with you, I want to share
a hand in hand hold with you,
I want to take off my coat when it's cold for you,
you've got me wanting to write one of those
over the top acoustic choruses,
"you're my sunshine on a rainy day, sweet raindrops on a sunny day,
my pain stops when you come my way, but
my brain rots when you run away"
but that's just not true,
I mean I care a lot for you, but you'll never
be the centre of my universe,
that place is taken by the One who's always
been the centre of the universe,
and I can't find my identity in the one I'm meant to be with,
though I'd love to find the identity of the one I'm meant to be with,
and if that one doesn't exist, is that something I can deal with?
I think I can,
because if I spend all my time searching for the 'perfect relationship'
I'll lose sight of the only perfect relationship I'll ever have,
but if the one I'm meant to be with is you?
honestly that'd be a dream come true,
I'd love to see you become more beautiful in your
seventies than you are in your twenties,
and I'd love us to be rich beyond our wildest dreams,
even if that means living in abject poverty,
because I believe in riches beyond just diamond bracelets,
and I believe in beauty beyond another facelift,
so I want to thank you for being the catalyst
for a thousand heartfelt words,
but most of all, I want to thank God, for
reminding me that I still believe in love.

Rael Mason

20. HENNINGHAM FAMILY PRESS

On live printmaking, making an alternative income and community-centered art

As a family-run collaborative bookbinding and printing outfit, David and Ping Henningham publish books and prints, do live printing shows, and execute commissions for clients. They are like a micro-brewery for books. Their work has been acquired by several key collections, including Chelsea College of Art, Tate Britain and UCLA. They have performed widely in the UK, several times in the London Word Festival, but most recently in the BBC Radio Theatre for *The Verb* with Ian McMillan, and also in Berlin, Ghent, Oslo and Bergen.

They work collaboratively producing work that varies wildly from rapid process-driven multiples through to painstakingly thorough deluxe editions in cloth-bound slipcases and many-layered, colourful prints. The written and graphic content is often generated through bespoke collaborative processes, and side-steps the categories of fiction and non-fiction, fitting the more general term 'writing', where all forms of text are given equal credit on the page.

This interview with David was conducted via email.

AG: Tell us about the early days of the Henningham Family Press. What made you decide to get into printing? How did you get started?

DH: We started the Henningham Family Press because Ping and myself wanted to work together and collaborate as much as we could with other artists. We were determined to make our living solely from our art, and provide for our family. We didn't have children at the time, but we wanted to structure our lives in such a way that we could be living successfully in an integrated way. So our press is an experiment in capitalism, a kind of guild. The workplace usually demands that it take a central position, but we wanted our family, our *domus,* to take that position. We also found the world of work unbelievably sexist. So, unlike the classical *domus,* within seconds of starting our own business we had equal opportunities for both genders. Strange how it is taking so long in Canary Wharf ...

Printing and bookbinding were perfect for us because it was easy to bring all our concerns together in book form: lectures, seminars, writing, graphic work, sculpture ... and it is more familiar to a wider audience than galleries. It is an alternative and integrated/cross-discipline exhibition space. Galleries are in acute need of revitalization but that looked like it would take a life's work to effect, and not the life's work we were interested in. The form of the work a person makes dictates the type and breadth of audience a person will have, as well as what their career path will feel like. Multiples are great for us because, instead of spending thousands of hours on one object, which demands a collector with thousands in the bank, we can sell hundreds of copies to hundreds of people and collaborate more freely.

AG: How did you make opportunities for the work back in the beginning? Not all art colleges give practical help for surviving as an artist after

graduation. Did you need to learn new skills? Where did you find help?

DH: By the time of my final show at the Slade we were very excited about getting on with it—I think we relished the experience of building things up, and the fact it is survival of the fittest kind of makes it more rewarding. We took what money we had to spend and what space we had to hand and built any equipment we couldn't afford. Our chipboard screen-printing table, with a door hinge and some g-clamps, paid for its aluminium replacement through profits. Artists are probably the only people who rent studio space without having a predictable income from their work, so we avoided that mistake. Family were very generous with space, but you can also work within the limitations of what you have at home. This reduces the part-time work that would be required to pay two rents. We made sure we wouldn't make a loss on our work: first projects had to pay for their material costs, and then we moved on to covering labour too. We planned very specific steps for moving from part-time work to full-time art. I got a part-time position as a bookbinding apprentice to learn more of those skills.

We filled in an Arts Council application and then shredded it. We didn't apply for any funding because, since John Major's government, almost all arts funding comes through the National Lottery. We realized this means that many of the poorest in society, who play the lottery in the hope they'll escape poverty, are subsidizing the work of middle-class artists who in many cases have two degrees but choose not to earn very much. This seems unacceptable to us. Another reason we tried so hard to pay our own way was that artists seem to have reversed the relationship between supply and demand. Artists want other people to supply their demand to be an artist. This we also found unacceptable—everyone should support themselves with their hands—and we find it hard to believe that God will free us up to sit in a studio all day and think only about our work; we must at some point be of use to other human beings. So we were open to

the ways in which our equipment and skills could help pay our way. Now about a third of our income is our own publications, a third our performance fees, and a third print and bind commissions we undertake for other people.

We put on about four events in the first year to promote our work, where we publicized them and did all the logistical work, and our friends very generously supported us and came to these. We suggest that people do this for up to two years and ensure that event promoters, publicity freelancers, journalists, anyone who would be interested in working with you over a long-term career, are coming to these events. If nobody starts offering you work in festivals, radio, press, or wherever it is you are aiming to work, then you probably need to rethink the structure of what you are doing. If you do good work, people with more experience than you will probably show you the ropes, but you need to collaborate further afield than just your mates from art school; too many shows are basically a school reunion. And of course the media you choose dictates how hard all this will be. If you want to be a painter with gallery representation then you have a lot of competition and more rigid conventions to negotiate. If you pick a niche then you have less competition, you make up the rules as you go, and survival is more likely. One isn't superior in value to the other, but it's best to go into it with your eyes open.

AG: I really enjoyed the event you organized in the East End a few months ago. It was an evening festival: a kind of village fair with art, music, lectures, village pub and stand-up comedy. A real collaborative event. Not just old college mates, as you describe it, but people from a variety of creative fields. For a lot of graduates it's trying to find the people to work with and make connections that will last. How did you build your network?

DH: Yes, that was 'Keep Printing and Carry On', an event put on by the London Word Festival. We were really buzzing during and after that experience. They basically wanted to put us in collaboration with as many people from as many disciplines as possible in one night. It's what we call 'performance publishing'; we made and sold three poster collaborations that night from the 'Chip Shop', our mobile silkscreen workshop. One each with Murray Macaulay, Joanna Neary and Darren Hayman. We love working with the London Word Festival guys. They are

kindred spirits, and we found that out by working with a lot of people who weren't similarly minded first, I suppose. But that trio found us through one of them seeing the Half-Handed Cloud show at the Foundry.

We structured the Henningham Family Press to be a family business, surrounded by an extended family of people we collaborate with. We expect a long-term relationship with collaboratees, and share our home and workshop with them at the time. We usually work with friends who are also interested in making something that is successful immediately, for the actual audience rather than the documentation. That's the main thing: a solid professional friendship is crucial; everything else flows from that. A group show is the opposite of a collaboration. A group show is like a Kellogg's variety pack, and collaboration is like a big box of Crunchy Nut Cornflakes: the honey and nuts actually work together and have something to say together. But I'm not saying that planning for the future is misguided. A lifetime of independently successful works that gradually improve in quality and sufficiency (for making a living wage, and daily sanity) is the goal, in my opinion. Maybe we just drink a lot with a lot of people? I can't think of anything we've done that didn't begin in a pub.

AG: What constitutes 'good work' for you and how do you know when you're making it?

DH: I suppose part of what you do at art school is work out the specific parameters for your work. We are aware of what our aims are for a project and if we achieve them. We show things to friends whose opinion we trust. If some people hate it and some other people love it then that's a good sign. There's a certain look on people's faces I'm looking for in a live show.

AG: What advice would you give to other artists starting out?

DH: We usually advise graduates to not make art on weekends. It is important to be idle, and when everyone else is. It gives you time to see friends and family, reflect on what you are doing, rest, do practical tasks that end up getting in the way on work days, keeps you in sync with the rest of society. This means looking for a part-time job of no more than three days a week, if you can get one.

Also, prioritize time actually spent on your artwork over things that merely make you look like an artist to other people. For example, it is better to work on your art at home three days a week rather than have a studio you can't afford unless you have a full-time job somewhere to pay for it. It is better to work within the constraints you have rather than feel this is some kind of compromise (after all, nobody seems to worry that it might be a compromise for their art to get bigger in their big MA studio...).

Finally, while you are trying to become a successful artist you might stumble across a job you never knew existed, like 'brain librarian' at a surgical museum, or casting monuments that will get flooded, or photographing the bottom of the sea, and you should take that job without feeling you've chickened out of being an artist. We're surprised that people who trained in art don't deliberately pursue more varied work; even something as regulated as the NHS has much more diversity in the jobs available. Being an artist means much more than getting a gallery to represent you or starting an artist-run gallery if they won't.

21. RACHEL NUNSON

On getting noticed in the design world, writing CVs and why going to parties is good for business

Rachel is Managing Director for an award-winning creative web agency that builds websites and smartphone and social-networking applications for major charities around the world. A former lecturer at the Hypermedia Research Centre at the University of Westminster, she has management and teaching experience on a variety of arts projects. She describes herself as a software artist with a sideways take on life and a love for building and sustaining creative community.

This interview was conducted as an email conversation over the course of three separate days.

AG: I was at a dinner party last week where someone asked me what I did. I always find that question tricky as there never seems to be a straightforward answer when you work in the arts or creative industries. How do you answer the question?

RN: I have exactly the same problem. I wish I had the guts to make up increasingly more ridiculous job titles ('I'm a flamingo tamer. I'm Jeremy Paxman's spittle guard. I'm a poshness technician for Cute Overload') to see which sparks off the most interesting conversation. It's hard to live in a culture where people are defined by what they do for money, and I'd like to think I'd be subverting that. I end up with something lame like 'I'm a creative type, but forget about my career: what are you passionate about?' A good friend of mine inspired me to do this and it's amazing what people begin to talk about when you focus the conversation onto what lights their fire rather than the 9 to 5 (or in my case, a fuzzy 10 or maybe 11 to between 6 and 9).

AG: I've tried that one sometimes too but I think I come across a bit intense. I tend to freak people out even more. Maybe I should stick with asking them what kind of fruit they'd like to be. Or what their favourite frozen animal is ... but passions: that's a good place to start. Let's go with that. What gets your creative juices flowing? What makes you want to design?

RN: I'm going to be brutally honest here. You might want to put on your crash helmet. There are times lately when I struggle to want to design. Responsibility can have quite a crushing effect on creativity, and clients, or (and perhaps especially) potential clients who turned you down can make you doubt yourself too. But when I think about it, new experiences, people, tastes, sounds or sights are what fire me up and make me want to design.

Um, frozen animal?

AG: How has the job changed for you as your career developed and you inherited greater responsibility?

RN: More stress and more excitement in equal measures. That said, it's been eleven years, and it's harder and harder to remember what it was like in the bad old days. Definitely less opportunity to be creative, because running a business is like having six children ... so many mouths to feed ... but it

is wonderful being a part of a team of very talented people. I much prefer it to working on my own, although when I worked on my own, I thought I preferred that to being part of a team. A lot better than 'the grass is always greener', I suppose.

AG: For a lot of graduates it can seem daunting starting out in the design world. If you could meet yourself starting out eleven years ago what advice would you give?

RN: I would say, firstly: You are capable of so much more than you think you are. And, secondly: When it gets tough (which it will), rather than doubting your calling or the decisions you've made, become obsessed with understanding the depths of God's love for you. Then the trust that you need to carry you through will well up out of you. Then the fear will seem like a little itch that only bothers you when you focus on it, rather than some sort of monster chasing you.

AG: Thinking about CVs and applying for jobs: you must have seen a fair few job applications as project director for Rechord. What do you look for in a new designer? Any tips for fresh faces on how to get yourself noticed?

RN: Bear in mind that this advice may not apply to other agencies, only to me, and my recruitment process is a little out of the ordinary, shall we say. I feel both sorry for and frustrated by creatives who lose their nerve when it comes to their CV, who send me a paint-by-numbers template filled with meaningless business vocabulary.

A CV is an advert for your skills, so use it to express yourself and give me a flavour of what kind of designer you are, in form as well as content. I like CVs that demonstrate personality, passion and achievements. Don't be shy. An online portfolio is crucial and should show the same qualities (at least, if you want to get a job at a web agency).

Finally, get somebody to proofread your CV and application. I know this sounds obvious, but it clearly isn't in practice, because a full 50 per cent of people who apply for jobs with Rechord don't do this. I got a covering letter recently that said, 'I'm conscientious when it comes to grammer and spelling.' I kid you not.

AG: Would you advise new designers to cold-contact design agencies? Does that ever work? If not, how do you get your foot in the door?

RN: Yes, definitely, do cold-contact design agencies. I always admire it when designers do that. Shows they have guts, and they really want to work for us, which is flattering. But preferably make your initial cold contact something nice ... *really nice* ... in the post. With chocolate. (OK, I'm sort of joking there.)

Follow it up with a phone call a few days later. Be persistent, charming and patient. Don't do the hard sell, though. Just say, 'Can I come over with my portfolio and have a chat?' and don't take 'no' for an answer. Agencies get *really* busy sometimes ... so keep calling (maybe once a fortnight) until you hit them at a moment of calm. Then just be yourself.

I know this works, because it worked for me when I needed to get a summer job, and it's worked *on* me as well.

Oh, and it's OK to be nervous. People like it when you are nervous about meeting them. It makes them feel more important, and it shows you really want to work for them. (Do you see a theme emerging here?)

AG: What should you put into your portfolio? Is it best to focus on what you think an agency wants to see, keep it broad, put in the stuff that's more about you: all or none of the above?

RN: Well, as much as I love to see the conceptual stuff, don't require me to make a leap of imagination to understand how your work might appeal to our clients. (Not because I have no imagination, but in all likelihood I'll be pretty tired and have a dozen other things on my mind when I see you.) Definitely throw in a piece that shows how clever and thoughtful you are, but do keep in a good amount of commercially applicable work. If you're applying for a job at a web agency, include at least two or three web layouts or interfaces. (Experimental commercial stuff is actually just fine.) Humour works especially well. Those portfolios that display a real sense of wit are always more memorable.

Here's one thing *not* to do: apologize. Some people are very defensive about their work and it's a bit painful. Even if you don't feel like it, at least try to appear proud. Smile. Tell me what your favourite work is and how it came to be. I like stories.

AG: Another possibility for new graduates is setting up your own business. What was it like for you

back in the early days of Rechord? How did you get started?

RN: I must be honest here ... I got started through sheer fluke. I was already in a quandary about where I should work, because I have a pretty sensitive conscience (although it is selectively sensitive sometimes! I'm sure I've got major ethical blind spots ...). I was concerned that if I got a job at an agency then, at some point, I'd have to choose between designing web stuff for a corporation with detestable business practices or my job. So that ruled out a lot of career options. But I hadn't seriously considered setting up my own business, apart from the spot of freelancing I'd done in summers between courses.

Shortly before the end of my postgrad, the chap with whom I'd collaborated closely in my final year at art college called me up and said, 'Do you want to set up a business together?' and I was so stunned I said 'yes' because I couldn't think of how to tell him 'no' in a polite way. But it was just as well, because we were almost instantly recognized by the industry (interviews in the design rags, awards and all that stuff), and he was fine about us turning down clients who didn't share our values.

That makes it sound easy but it was hard. Very hard. In the early days I barely had enough money to feed myself, and used to eat breakfast from the blackberry bush that grew outside our office. Every £1 earned was a triumph. Every new contract, however small, made us feel elated. It was wonderful working with Stefan in those times because he'd been in business before, and, despite not sharing my faith, he had more confidence than I did that God would provide for us. And he did. So that was a lesson in perseverance.

AG: How did your Christian faith influence the decisions you were making at the time?

RN: My faith definitely influenced my decision to turn down a five-figure-sized project for a major international bank. It could have been a big break for us, but I felt that aiming to be Christ-like was incompatible with working for an organization that (in my view) oppressed the poor, and I persuaded Stef it was the right thing to do. Thankfully, he agreed. This turned out to be for the best, because if we'd gotten involved with the project, we wouldn't have been able to produce some bespoke work for the Creative Futures exhibition (as we'd just won an award). That in turn led to a five-figure-sum piece of work (although substantially smaller) and we've been able to mention the Creative Futures award ever since.

I'm getting a bit off-topic there, but without my faith, I would never have had the strength to take that kind of risk. It also shaped the whole image, nature and method of doing business … We were determined to reject business practices we saw as being harmful to creation or people, and start entirely new ones that we thought would make our work, and working life, better.

AG: Any tips for grads looking to set themselves up independently as a business? Where do you start? Where can you get help?

RN: It's been over ten years since I had to do this, so I'm not sure how the landscape of business support has changed, but Business Link was my first port of call, and through them I got access to a free two-day course on setting up your own business (which was invaluable, as there are so many rules and regulations) and eventually a grant to buy some new computer equipment and other bits and bobs. My university also ran a business start-up support scheme, and a lot of universities are being encouraged (by which I mean, goaded with a sharp stick) to help graduates start up in business. This is known in academia as 'Knowledge Transfer' and it's very trendy at the moment in government/EU funding programmes, so it may be the best way to get the support you need. Other than that, go to lots of parties. Seriously! Expanding your group of friends is one of the best ways to meet the right people who will help your business grow, whether that's through emotional, financial or physical support. Or being the person who connects you to the all-important funder or partner.

AG: Thanks, Rachel. That's been a real help and good fun talking to you.

22. SPARKS

On the cold face of design, taking the long view and turning principle into practice

Sparks is a design studio based in East London. It is run by Michael Gough and Gary McIlwaine. Gary studied Visual Communication at the University of Ulster and started working in a design studio in Belfast. He came to London to work for a new media company in 1999 and established Sparks as a professional design studio in 2003. Michael studied Fine Art at Norwich School of Art. Before establishing Sparks, he spent nine years working in the charity sector while continuing to develop his art.

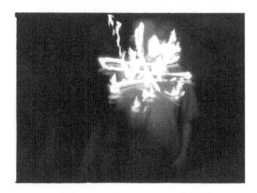

AG: Who and what are Sparks? How did the group begin and how has it evolved through the years?

This interview was conducted as an email conversation with Michael and Gary.

M&G: Sparks began in 1999. Initially we started out as a think-tank: that's an excuse for a group of mates that wanted to hang out and talk. Most of us were graduates whose paths had crossed as students at the UCCF Interface gatherings. We met once a month to go to exhibitions or lectures, show our recent work and generally encourage each other as we started out in our professional careers. The desire was to keep thinking about the themes we had come across at Interface, but in a professional context.

We were spurred on by an essay by Calvin Seerveld, 'The Freedom and Responsibility of the Artist' [from *Bearing Fresh Olive Leaves*], where he points to great divides in contemporary Christianity and contemporary art practice. He suggested there was a great deal to do by those who were trying to engage with the creative industries and warned about shrinking into a subculture. Helpfully, he suggested a few practical ideas. We thought there was enough writing and thinking on these issues and it was time to try it out.

Initially there were twelve of us, from a range of creative disciplines: architecture, fine art, interactive and product design, to name a few. Opportunities came up to create some work together; most were exhibitions but some design commissions were coming in too. We were also influenced by high-profile art and design collectives like Tomato and Fuel, so working on projects that crossed disciplines got us really excited.

The people whom we found ourselves working with were either charities or musicians who were trying to do something different, and didn't want to conform to the subculture or industry stereotypes that surrounded them. Because we had so much of Seerveld's thinking in our blood, we developed a bit of a niche for understanding that distinction.

In 2003 we saw an increase in our design commissions and took the opportunity to develop Sparks into a 'proper' design studio. A few of us gave up our day jobs to do this; we worked in spare rooms, bedrooms and on kitchen tables and started going out looking for projects rather than waiting for them to arrive.

Today Sparks is first and foremost a design studio, working with artists, businesses and charities. Our strength is in working with organizations and people who are doing something different in their industry and want to appear

distinctive and relevant. We have a studio of four to five regulars and a host of freelancers and collaborators whom we work with, depending on the requirements of the project.

AG: How do you make opportunities for the work and what makes for an interesting project?

M&G: Amongst other things we're currently working on some bespoke packaging for a limited-edition release of a new album for an artist signed to RCA records, a brand identity for a new management consultancy company, some school-based lesson plans and handbooks for eleven– to sixteen-year-olds about entrepreneurship, for a charity.

The best projects tend to be with clients who are looking for something very distinct from their peers or something that will stand out in the culture that they are working in. Typically it would be a company who are trying to be, do or create something new within an existing industry: a musician trying to avoid clichés of the record industry or a charity wanting to engage young people in real-life issues. We get a lot of satisfaction thinking up alternative ways to solve a particular and possibly familiar design problem.

AG: What books, people, resources helped formulate your understanding of design in the early days?

M&G: That's interesting, as one of us studied graphic design at college and the other came at it later from a fine art background; the influences and resources have been many and quite varied. We were both at college during the 90s: David Carson, Neville Brody, The Face, 4AD records and the YBA art movement were really popular.

The strong collaborative ethos in the early days of Sparks has really shaped our thinking; we were all mates, but coming together from many backgrounds. Learning how an architect, sculptor and painter approached their work also impacted how we each approached our own work. In that sense, I guess we were 'of our time', in that boundaries around disciplines were disappearing in the educational establishments; that was carried through to working practice too. Tomato were the pinnacle of that generation, and doing lots of interesting work, gaining popularity and recognition through the band Underworld. We looked to them a

lot; they helped us put a plausible case together for what we were trying to do, although our truer motivation was in Seerveld's writing.

When we began meeting together at weekends, we asked people to come and give a lecture or lead a discussion: Nigel Halliday, Norman Fraser, Tony Watkins, Wade Bradshaw, Andrew Fellows, Marcus Honeysett. None are graphic designers, but they were all interested in what we were attempting and, consciously or unconsciously, have shaped our thinking. Their insight as writers, historians, theologians and critics, at a high level, has been invaluable, although sometimes overwhelming.

AG: How do ideas discussed by theologians, writers and critics work their way into what goes on in the studio?

M&G: It's a hard thing to try and measure, but it would affect the way we conceive and discuss the relative appropriateness of our concepts in response to a brief. The ideas tend to come out in the discussion we have as a group in reflecting on our work.

AG: You mentioned the importance of Seerveld's writing in the early days of Sparks. What principles inform your practice now? How does being a Christian shape your approach to running a design agency?

M&G: Most of Seerveld's writings are set in the context of a fine-art practitioner, so we've always had to do some translation to think what it means for commercial graphic design. We'd like to maintain that, as with any fine artist, creativity is at our core. The skills, techniques and understanding of working with a visual language all need to be developed and constantly honed. Seerveld took the 'long view' on this, noting that apart from a few lone exceptions, Christians and the Christian subculture were lagging far behind contemporary standards and had a lot of work to do to re-engage with contemporary culture. Discouragingly he talked about it taking one or two generations of second-rate practitioners to catch up. So one of his principles is that it will be hard work; there are no quick or easy routes and there is much sweating and grafting to be done.

Another concerns the content of the work that is made. Seerveld makes a helpful distinction between pursuing and creating work that is relevant rather than popular. He challenges the practitioner to think hard about what kind of work is needed by culture and warns against working to always meet the expectations of the audience. For our studio activity this means presenting a couple of different routes to a client: perhaps one that works loosely within the client's expectations and then another that challenges the assumptions the client has about the project.

In a commercial design studio, there is a much clearer client and supplier distinction than in other art practices; on many levels it's not that different to any other business in a service industry. There are also employees and the working environment to manage; money and cash flow to look after; negotiations, agreements and contracts to honour. Seerveld didn't write so much about these things, but fortunately the Bible has plenty to say about being good stewards. It has many warnings about the pitfalls of money and advice about how to act with integrity. We are constantly challenged to be as rigorous with these principles along with our creative principles.

In business practice, as in creative practice, there are constant temptations to be lazy, to be dishonourable and to make the most of any opportunity to inflate your own ego or profit margin. On the other hand, to keep doing what we do, we need to look for and convince people to work with us, negotiate the right terms and carry out the work effectively. There are many times when judgement has been skewed by our own weaknesses and temptations. We value that Sparks is a partnership, and try to keep each other in check. If we are not accountable at that level, it would be very easy to give in and think of things only in the very short term.

AG: Read/seen/heard anything good recently? Anything you'd recommend to new designers?

M&G: Today, we read the usual industry rags—*Creative Review* etc.—but lots of that can be self-congratulatory and insular so needs to be taken with a pinch of salt. *Eye* has very good writing, with articles that are much better at contextualizing current and past work. Adrian Shaughnessy wrote a great book *How to Be a Graphic Designer without Losing Your Soul* (no spiritual content), which every design student should read before they leave college. We have been to some great D&AD lectures, Lance

Wyman and Milton Glaser among the highlights. Last year we took the studio to a design conference in Dublin called Offset. We got to listen to Massimo Vingelli, who was truly refreshing; it was great to see work created 30 years ago that looks as relevant and contemporary today. It is well worth reading a little book called *Art Needs No Justification* by Hans Rookmaaker and also *Being Human* by Ranald Macaulay and Jerram Barrs, if you can lay your hands on them.

AG: For many of our graduates there's a struggle between matching the ideology of working as a Christian with the reality of working at the cold face of the creative industries. I can hear this tension as you talk about issues of cash flow, negotiations, looking after employees and honouring contracts.

M&G: We'd certainly sympathize with that struggle, and also say that the first few years out of college are really formative. The ideals, intentions and ambitions of a graduate usually become weakened over time, rather than become stronger. There is a very real temptation to give in to one culture or another. For example, it's easy to be completely absorbed by your creative practice, and let your faith and beliefs be put on hold until you've made it. Or, if you are a 'good' Christian, are involved in your church, show some interest in theology, display signs of pastoral or evangelistic gifts, then there is usually a huge pull from that culture to put artistic practice on hold and use your gifts to serve that community. Both responses are detrimental; they serve to widen the gap between the cultures, and make it even harder for either to engage.

AG: Where is the tension felt most for Sparks? What encourages you to keep integrity?

M&G: For us, after ten years, those tensions are still there; it would be more comfortable to retract to one corner or the other. However, currently, the temptation is for us to place too much emphasis on the creative work we do or the commercial success of the studio and make either one into an idol or mini-god. We like to do good work and want recognition for what we do, but at the same time we need it to be commercially viable. Those two desires often pull us in opposite directions and are the source of most tensions. Of course, both desires are not in themselves wrong, but either can overtake our ambitions and start to skew the decisions that we make.

Again, we're thankful that Sparks is a partnership, and although that means that it may take us a bit longer to make decisions, that time is useful for checking motivation and intentions.

Over the years we've also tried to build good relationships with people outside Sparks to be accountable to. We often take a day out and go to L'Abri in Hampshire: have a little reflection, chat with folks a lot wiser and more experienced than us and make some plans for the future. We wish we could say that our local church helps us in that accountability too, but we are not sure that it has the responsibility to understand the intricacies of every member's vocation: that would be quite demanding. But there are good friendships within that community that help with general accountability and encourage us to keep integrity.

All that said, we still get it wrong far too often.

AG: How do you know when you're making good work?

M&G: We enjoy listening to music, seeing shows, talking with people about their aims in business or in charitable endeavours, and then thinking about what is an appropriate creative or visual response. If we can create something that helps them achieve what they need, maybe even push them to be a bit more distinct and creative, then we take great pleasure in that.

We're really satisfied at the end of a project if we can put it in our portfolio, and show it to colleagues and clients without making excuses or apologies. If we have to put it in that drawer that is reserved for the projects that have gone wrong, then we are disappointed.

AG: When you look back on Sparks studio practice in ten years' time, what will make you say 'job well done'?

M&G: In terms of studio practice, if 'collaboration' was the buzzword ten years ago, then the word 'sustainability' is the current one. Everybody's using it. We're keen that Sparks is around in some form or other in the next ten years. Over the past few years we've established that we can do 'it', but it has been with the patience and support of very gracious wives and families. We are currently trying to work out how to keep going, maintain marriages, develop a good studio working environment and build up some level of financial security that will allow us to build a wider team to share the load and responsibility. Apart from the day-to-day projects, that is our current challenge.

In light of Seerveld's essay and the history of Sparks, if in another ten years' time we were classed by the historians and critics as anything above second-rate practitioners, then we'd smile.

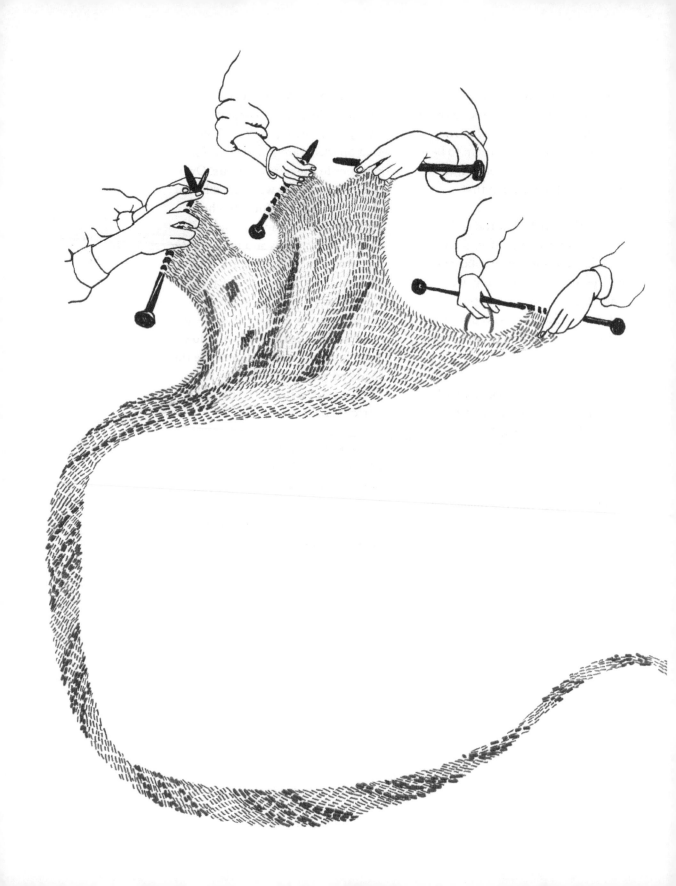

Life after Art College

Introduction

Many artists find the first years after art college are the most turbulent of their career. Finances may be tight, opportunities aloof and the old support networks of college missing. But it's not all doom and gloom. If you're willing to put in the extra work and seek out opportunities these early years might also be the most rewarding.

Recent graduates often find unique opportunities that don't repeat later in life such as specific graduate funding, awards, residencies and travel scholarships. As such you may enjoy freedom to learn new skills, explore alternative careers, meet new people, move location with perhaps few expectations, commitments or responsibilities to other employees, church and family.

As I write, in 2010, the government has announced a substancial increase in university tution fees. It is therefore likely student debt will rise and pressure on graduates to find work soon after studies will increase. The government have also announced funding cuts for the arts, which will put greater financial stress on arts graduates.

In this short section we will discuss some pragmatic issues you might face as an emerging artist. Where will you find work? How will you build a network? Who will pay the rent? When will you find stability in your career? How will you continue to serve Christ? These two chapters won't address all the issues, but I hope they will offer some framework for you within which to work out what needs to happen next. It concludes with a final short resources section.

23. Making and Managing Opportunities in Visual Art

I hate to sound like a romantic adolescent, but I believe artists don't generally see art as a career choice, they simply can't overcome their desire to make art, and will live on little income for as long as they have to, before they start to sell their work—or give up and get a paying job ... There's a ten per cent chance you will end up with a 'career', but in the meantime you should have fun, make friends and be inspired to make a go of something in the art world.

Charles Saatchi, art collector[34]

At some point the awful truth hits you. No one is coming to get you, to beat down a path to your door. You have to go and get them and it's going to take guts and flair.

Diana Hudson, artist and business advisor[35]

This chapter is an accumulation of advice from professional artists including Luci Metcalfe, Kaori Homma, Robert Orchardson and tutors at the University of the Arts, London. I thank them for their help and acknowledge their influence in shaping these ideas.

Making the most of your degree show

The final year show is your chance to shine as an artist and show the world what you're made of. It's the accumulation of three years' work with family, friends and tutors all coming together at the same time in what many students experience as the most unsettling collision of worlds. If you have made contacts before your final year, the degree show can be a great way to invite them back to see how your work has developed and this can sometimes lead to good things, and new contacts made during the week itself can sometimes bear fruit. It's a very exciting time but it can also feel like a lot of pressure. It's important to prepare well, not just in the work but also mentally and in prayer.

I don't want to burst the bubble but it's important to have realistic expectations about your degree. For most art students the degree show is not the launch pad of career that they hope for. It's quite unlikely that Charles Saatchi will see your show or that a major gallery will buy up all your work. There are things you can do, however, that will help you to make the most of the week.

34. My Name Is Charles Saatchi and I Am an Artoholic *(London: Phaidon Press, 2009), page unknown.*

35. *Quoted from her article 'Creating and Managing Opportunities in the Visual Arts' in the* Arts Centre Group Mentoring Project Handbook *(2003), p. 21.*

It's all about making yourself visible. Take a bit of time to *design business cards* with your contact information. If you are wanting to sell work have a list of prices easily accessible as this prevents a little awkwardness and you may get more interest if the audience know you mean business.

It's very important that you *be there* through the week. There's no point complaining that no one came to see your work if you weren't there to oversee the show.

Have *a notebook for people to leave comments and contact details*. This isn't just for your own encouragement but might lead to good contacts to follow up later. When the dust settles on the show, make sure you call any galleries who left their details or go round to see them to politely remind them of who you are.

A friend of mine paid for a fleet of taxis to bring gallery owners from around London to his MA degree show. This was a great way for him to put himself on their radar.

After the degree show

Careers in the arts don't fall from trees but there are ways of making opportunities for yourself after art college that don't necessarily involve the end of the dole queue. The most successful artists ten years down the line aren't necessarily those who got the best results at the degree show. It's often those who just stick at it, work hard and who know how to promote themselves who will still be working as artists in the years to come. Very few galleries will ask what grade you got for your degree but they will be interested in what you have done since graduation.

Your degree work will not be the strongest work of your career but rather a launch pad from which you bounce to greater things.

Building a network

There are very few artists today who work in isolation. Most artists find it beneficial to be *part of a community or network* of some kind in which ideas can be exchanged, contacts swapped, resources shared, critique given and where they can find others to work on art projects with them and exhibit together. *Keep in touch* with friends from art college and let them know what you're up to as the years go by. Get yourself a studio space in an artists' community or communal studios. Most cities have artists' studios that will put on shared open-studio days when your work can be exposed to others who wouldn't normally get to see it.

There are good *online networks* you can join, such as www.artnet.com and www.artrabbit.com. Facebook and MySpace are excellent tools for organizing art projects and letting people know what you're up to.

Make the effort to go to *private views and gallery openings*, especially of the galleries you would like to exhibit with in the future. Don't be a wallflower. Most curators like to talk about the work on the walls so talk to them about the work, the gallery, what else is on at the moment and what's coming up next. Many graduate artists make the mistake of talking about themselves all the time with gallery owners but this strategy rarely bears fruit in the long run. It's much better to show a genuine interest in the art of others as it shows an understanding of why you do what you do, suggesting that you have thought critically about how your own practice fits into the wider scene.

Many graduating artists find it helpful to find a cluster of friends to go to private views together. It can be an intimidating experience to walk into a gallery full of the art elite on your own, although I find I am more likely to pluck up the courage to talk to people I don't know if I am on my own. There will be others on their own too and it's perfectly OK to begin a conversation about the art without freaking people out. Just be polite, inquisitive and casual, be careful how much you drink and don't stuff your face with the garlic prawns.

Finding and making work

Most artists need to find part-time work to subsidize their studio practice. *Gallery or art-technician work* can be a good way of keeping in the loop with others in a similar situation. If you can find other ways of paying the rent it helps to take an *unpaid internship with a gallery*, especially if you want to go down the curatorial route in the future.

Teaching is a very good option and many graduates find it wise to complete a PGCE shortly after their first degrees. Some schools and colleges see the value in art teachers being practitioners and operate part-time schemes for teachers who want to continue their own art practice whilst teaching.

You know what kind of work will suit you best in allowing you the time, finances and energy to keep making art. There's no point working long hours to subsidize your art if it means you have no mental energy left over at the end of the day to paint. It might be that you need to take a less demanding job or work fewer hours and cut back on spending elsewhere.

It's rare for a graduating student to be given an offer of a solo exhibition straight off the back of their degree show but you can get there if you put in the groundwork of *applying for awards, group exhibitions and artist residencies*. Much of the artist's time is spent filling in application forms and writing letters but be careful not to spend so much time in applications that you have no work to show in your portfolio. Magazines like *a-n* have regular lists of job vacancies, residencies and competitions you can apply for. I've also found *The Artists' Yearbook*, published annually by Thames & Hudson, to be an invaluable resource, especially for funding bodies and trusts. There's a real trick in knowing which *funding* body to apply to for which project and much time can be spared if you do your homework before applying cold to a trust fund.

If there's nothing in the diary and no apparent opportunities for your work just organize one yourself. Much of the most dynamic exhibiting I have experienced was born out of frustration at the lack of artist opportunities. You could, for example, turn your flat into a temporary gallery, hire out a project space with friends or look for cheaper venues such as derelict shops, warehouses and empty office blocks. Sarah Lucas and Tracey Emin launched their careers during the 1990s recession out of a series of self-promoted exhibitions at the redundant City Racing betting shop in London's East End. Sometimes it's about turning a frustrating scenario to your favour with a bit of lateral thinking and hard graft.

Making a plan

The key to surviving as an artist after art college isn't necessarily the ability to make good art. As artist and business advisor Diana Hudson puts it,

> Surviving as a professional artist will involve acquiring and maintaining professional skills. The world does not owe you a living nor does it arrive uninvited on your doorstep. To be effective it is important to understand your special

abilities and limitations. For some, the very idea of being good at business is quite distasteful and will at best stifle creativity. But this business thing is about being professional as an artist; it is about giving yourself a fair chance and not shooting yourself in the foot.[36]

It's good to ask yourself where you would like to be in five, ten or twenty years' time. Would you like to be making art? Would you like to teach? Do you see yourself travelling, getting married, having a family? We don't know exactly what life will bring us but the answer to these kinds of questions will influence the plans you make for the future and the way you invest your time and resources now.

The first thing to do is work out your *budget*. You don't need to have a degree in accountancy to calculate how much money you will need to survive monthly and what your average spending will be. Take a blank sheet of paper and write out what you need for rent, tax and bills. Look down your bank statements from previous months and calculate your average expenditure on food, clothes, entertainment, art materials and other regular expenses. This will

give you a realistic idea of the level of income you are used to. Factor in any course fees or training you will need over the coming months and work out whether your income matches your outgoing expenses.

Getting out of debt

Most students inevitably have a bit of *debt* when they leave art school and paying it off can be a daunting prospect. Try not to panic but be realistic in how much money you need to set aside each month to pay off the loan. When you've been in a situation in which you are dependant on loans to survive as a student it can be easy to get used to living in debt, but this kind of mindset can be catastrophic for your future and career. Aside from the biblical warnings about the consequences of debt, debt can cripple creativity. Opportunities can pass you by because you just can't afford them, and you may not even be able to afford the materials you need.

Debt is not inevitable. Avoid using *credit cards* as much as possible and don't get yourself into more debt by paying for things on credit. A friend of mine avoids credit and debit cards altogether. Every Monday morning she withdraws her weekly budget from

36. *As above.*

the bank as cash and simply lives out of her wallet from day to day. This way she knows exactly how much she has left for the rest of the week and has learned to economize her spending at the beginning of the week so that she can splash out at the weekends.

I've found it useful to have three bank *accounts for separate expenditures*. The first account is for daily spending such as food, cinema and evenings out. The second is for bills and rent (I calculated how much my bills came to in an average month and set up a direct debit for that amount from my main account at the beginning of the month. That way I knew exactly how much money I had left over for the rest of the month, could budget ahead and didn't have to worry about when the next bill would come out and how much it would be). My third account is for art materials and art projects which I top up whenever I sell work or have extra income.

Once you've worked out your financial situation you are free to plot and plan about art projects. If you have an art budget of £30 per month you will not be able to work on six-foot canvases every morning. You might need to adjust your working methods until you get more funding. If there's a project you really want to go for, like an overseas research trip or major installation, you need to plan ahead and raise funds for that in advance. An artist who shows initiative in measure with responsibility will be more attractive to potential clients than someone who is erratic and unpredictable in their approach.

Making opportunities

Opportunities for your art will not fall from the sky into your lap. You will need to set aside time in your working week to *initiate projects and look for opportunities*. Art magazines such as *a-n* and websites such as www.artrabbit.com and www.artnet. com have regular listings of artists' residencies, awards and other job opportunities for artists.

It's useful to have an *online portfolio* you can point potential clients and galleries towards. Make the time to visit other artists who are doing what you'd like to be doing in the future. Ask them what steps they took to get there. You might be able to offer yourself as a *studio assistant* for a period with them. Do you want to work with galleries or outside the art markets? The more you can focus your aims the greater your chance of success as you spend less time pursuing opportunities you really don't need and are free to spend precious studio time on more worthwhile ventures.

To MA or not to MA?

A *postgraduate qualification* can open new possibilities for expanding your working practice or focusing on one particular area. With so many artists graduating from art college these days a further qualification can look good on your CV and certainly improve your options for work in education. It's important to pick the right MA, though. Different colleges offer different options for study and some courses may be more highly regarded than others by those you want to be working with in the future. *Do your research* and don't default to an MA just because you can't think of anything else to do. A postgraduate qualification is not a golden ticket to a glittering career in the arts. Think about why you want to do an MA. Which Masters course will best suit you and what you want to achieve from it?

Keep going

Whatever happens, don't give up! It can take years to establish a grounded career in the arts. Keep

your options open. There is more than one way to use a degree in art and I'm often surprised at how few arts graduates look for careers that don't involve waiting on blue-chip galleries to finally return their calls. An arts education should equip you with a way of seeing, measuring and processing the world that is a good foundation for any job that involves thinking outside the box or creative practice. Of my 32 year-group peers at art college I am aware of three who are now represented by galleries in Glasgow and London: two have switched to curating and one has opened his own gallery. Most of our group are now working in careers outside visual arts markets. One is a journalist for a local paper, five are teaching, one takes photographs of the ocean floor for an international engineering corporation and another makes prosthetic limbs. There is more than one way to use an arts degree.

For those who want to keep making art, in whatever context, in years to come it is important to saturate yourself in the arts. *Go and see as much art as possible; talk to those who make it, curate it and sell it; read about it as often as you can; and keep making it.* I have a friend who has made a drawing every day for nearly ten years and it's no surprise that his draughtsmanship is now remarkable. *Keep a sketchbook or notebook to journal ideas.* No idea is wasted as each one can inform the next. Some will be left on the back burner whilst others may become the work of your career.

Above all, keep going. Some of us will earn a living from our work and others will make a living so that we can make art. Whether you exhibit in the Tate or round the kitchen table with your children it is important to remember that your acts of creativity have value in the Kingdom of God and should challenge, encourage and bring great pleasure to yourself and to those around you. This, in turn, brings great delight to the Author of all creativity himself.

Q: Take a moment to reflect on your current practice. What skills, opportunities or ideas do you need to develop?

Q: What help do you need to develop your career? Where can you get that help?

Q: Where do you see yourself in five years time? What needs to happen next to help you get there?

24. Making and Managing Opportunities in the Performing Arts

by Sue Beresford

This chapter is an updated version of the article 'Creating and Managing Opportunities in the Performing Arts' originally written by Susan Beresford for *The Arts Centre Group Mentoring Handbook* (2003). It is used with permission. Susan Beresford is an actor and professional voice coach.

The various challenges which face anyone wishing to pursue a career in performing arts in the 21st century are, not surprisingly, very similar to the ones I faced when I joined the acting profession over thirty years ago. There are still too many of us competing for too few jobs and many of those jobs, particularly in theatre, are still poorly paid compared to the average wage. In fact, if you are doing a profit share, you may not even be paid at all! But a passion for the performing arts cannot be dampened by gloomy statistics and if we are Christians, our motivation is to perform for the love of God. We are on stage, or in front of the camera, because the love of God has called us to be there.

However, if we are called we also have to be committed and that requires a large amount of determination and perspiration along with the inspiration! In order to create opportunities you will need to be practical, disciplined and imaginative. Casting directors do not work by osmosis—they will only know you exist if you tell them. Your first introduction will usually be by CV and photograph.

Your *CV* is a history of your life in art. It reduces many hours of work, sweat, tears, joys and sorrows to a few words on a piece of paper. A CV serves two basic functions:

When you are not present, your CV tells a producer, director, or casting director about your experience. It can show whether your career has thus far had a classical bias, is mainly in musical theatre or is mostly in television. Essentially your experience on your CV serves as a guide as to what you've done and in what direction your career has headed to date.

When you go for an *interview* your CV serves as a kind of instant aid to communication. You may have worked with a director your interviewer knows or a writer they particularly admire. This can act as a springboard to further discussion and open up the interview.

What should you put into a CV and what should you leave out? Firstly, it should have your name, address, email and a phone number where you can be reached. If you have an agent, their name and telephone number should also be included and if your photograph is in Spotlight, the page and pin numbers should be given. Include your height, eye and hair colour, your playing age and the training you have had.

After that, the CV should contain nothing more or less than a brief outline of what you've done, where you've done it, and who directed it. Don't make it over-long. I would always advise keeping it to one A4 sheet. Casting directors do not have the time to wade through pages and pages of an actor's life history. I've worked in that capacity and I speak from experience! Make your CV clear and concise and don't be afraid to prune it. University and drama school productions can be deleted as you have more professional credits to add. It is best to separate the categories of work—i.e. theatre credits, film and television credits, radio, virals and commercials and corporate work—and put your most recent work first.

Include any specialist skills such as driving, sports, acrobatics, stage fighting, along with any languages. Accents and dialects should be listed separately as should your singing range and dancing ability.

Your *covering letter* enclosing your CV and *photograph* will give you the opportunity to point out the relevant areas of work which may be of interest to a potential employer. Proofread everything you are sending for spelling and ensure you have been accurate with names. If you are emailing the information, check that this is acceptable to reduce the risk of your submission being treated as spam and also ensure that it is in a file format that is easy to open. It's a good idea to email it to yourself first to make sure that it opens properly before sending it out.

What about your photographs? Quite simply, these photographs should look like you. You as you are right now. Do choose a photographer whose work you really like. Check with other actors and look at their pictures. As well as being clear and interesting, more importantly do they really look like the actor they represent? Have they captured the essence of that personality?

And remember, when you go for your photographic session, do prepare yourself thoroughly beforehand—not just what you're going to wear and how your hair will look, but also your mind and your feelings. If someone really wants their picture taken, it's usually easy to get a good picture of them.

Don't forget to put your name, agent's details if you have one, together with your height, eye and hair colour on the back of your photograph. Photographs can become separated from CVs and if your name is not on your picture the casting director will have no idea who you are!

Many of you will, I'm sure, already be familiar with Spotlight and the casting opportunities that are available to performers through advertising in their casting directory. As a Spotlight member you receive a CV on spotlight.com which is a web page with your CV, featuring your photos, voice and video clips, which is available to thousands of casting professionals working in stage, TV, commercials and film. You will also have your picture in the *Spotlight* books which are used daily by casting professionals worldwide. They will also offer advice on a one-to-one basis on photos, CVs or career development and the Spotlight card will give you exclusive discounts on a wide variety of products and services. They have also produced

a series of podcasts to provide members with useful career advice. You can get the latest episodes automatically by subscribing to the Spotlight Podcast in iTunes.

On their website, Spotlight cites that in the year to April 2010, an average of 198 casting breakdowns were sent out each week via The Spotlight Link, spanning every type of performance work: from TV to dance, film to live events, commercials to musicals. These contained an average of 483 individual roles every week. If you are without an agent and are c/o Spotlight you will receive relevant job information daily by email and can submit your Spotlight web CV instantly for all suitable roles. If you have an agent they will have access to this exclusive casting service.

Check out the Spotlight website www.spotlight.com for further information on all the services available.

Another *online directory* of professional actors, presenters, agents and casting professionals is Casting Call Pro, which currently has 20,000+ industry professionals on their system. Casting Call Pro offers free standard membership to all professional actors. This gives you a completely free listing in their actors directory of actors used regularly by casting and industry professionals. As well as the free directory listing and the casting call alert service, Casting Call Pro has a very active community and networking element, and a whole host of online resources to help you in your career. Again, check out their website www.castingcallpro.com for further information.

So what about the practical business of finding work. How do you find out what's going on and who is casting what? As well as the resources available through Spotlight and Casting Call Pro, casting information is available to benefit Equity members on their website www.equity.org.uk and is updated on a regular basis. Many theatre companies have their own websites on which they list their forthcoming seasons. The Royal Exchange Theatre in Manchester has a very comprehensive listing of all available casting on their website www.royalexchangetheatre.org.uk. Jobs and auditions are also advertised in the weekly publication *The Stage*. This is available online at www.thestage.co.uk and also has a very helpful advice section on their Jobs and Auditions page.

Get in the habit of looking closely at the credits at the end of a film or television programme to note who

has cast it. Of course it's also worth noting who produced and directed it. If you are up for a casting with that particular director it's always helpful if you can comment on their work. They are human too and need affirmation just as much as you do!

Some *casting directors* still hold general interviews and it may be worth phoning and/or writing to enquire about this. This is a case of 'suck it and see' to find out who are the ones most amenable to this approach.

Contacts, which is published by Spotlight, is a valuable reference directory which includes lists of agents, film, TV and theatre companies together with a full list of casting directors. It also gives details of photographers with examples of their work. It is updated each year and is a handy source of information.

If you're currently appearing on stage or TV, this offers an excellent opportunity to invite casting directors, agents and directors to see your work. If you also have a showreel of your work mention it in your letter and if it is available to view on your Spotlight page and on Casting Call Pro let them know.

Don't leave it to the last minute to invite them as they receive many invitations; it is a good idea to try to give, say, three weeks' notice. You don't need to give them masses of information—they won't have time to read it! A letter giving details of the play, the part or parts you are playing, venue, dates, times etc. is perfectly acceptable. Enclose a flyer as well if you have one. Travel directions are also helpful, especially if it is an out-of-town venue. It's also good practice to offer them a complimentary ticket although in most cases such 'comps' are usually available for this purpose.

Regarding *agents*, it is the norm to only have one to represent you in most fields of the performing arts; the exceptions being having a separate agent to represent you for voiceover work, modelling and commercials. Having more than one agent should only be with the knowledge, consent and agreement of all concerned.

Choosing an agent takes time, patience and skill. It can sometimes be compared to finding the right partner in marriage, although I'm not suggesting you fall in love with your agent! Do remember that such relationships are two-way but also remember that you are employing your agent to represent you. I don't

concur with the view of some who say you should change your agent every two or three years; if you have a good relationship stay with them. There is certainly no point in changing agents every five minutes for the sake of it (even supposing you could). In any case, it does not reflect well on you if you have had a succession of agents and you might also consider the view that you are simply changing deckchairs on the *Titanic!*

You need to be choosing an agent who can represent you in the area of work you want to pursue—some agents specialize in musical theatre, for example, while others cover TV, film and theatre. You may also consider actors' cooperative agencies which are run by actors themselves; typically 15–25 actors who act as each other's agent on a rota basis. This can give you a greater feeling of control over your career but does entail a lot of work.

I have only begun to scratch the surface in this article. It may sound a cliché but it's true that the more work you do the more you will learn about how to get work. When you're in work, ask questions and get advice from other actors. You might consider joining the Actors Centre in order to continue your professional development. They run approximately 1700 classes and workshops a year and it's worth checking out their website www. actorscentre.co.uk for further information.

If you are out of work don't despair. I realize you will probably have to take a temporary job in order to survive financially but that doesn't mean you can't usefully use the spare time you have. *Read plays on your tube journey to work. Learn some new audition speeches. Go to the theatre. Keep abreast of new writing. Start gathering material you enjoy performing.* You never know, it might be something you can develop into a one-person show one day. If you have difficulty sight reading and this has let you down at previous auditions, make it a task for five minutes each day to read a piece of text out loud. Keep practising, keep persevering and never lose that passion!

For we are God's workmanship, created in Christ Jesus to do good works, which God prepared in advance for us to do. (Eph 2:10)

Q: Take a moment to reflect on your current practice. What skills, opportunities or ideas do you need to develop?

Q: What help do you need to develop your career? Where can you get that help?

Q: Where do you see yourself in five years time? What needs to happen next to help you get there?

That Oddity of Being Evangelical and Artist

An Interval

Contemporary Art, I think, is as far from organized religion as Western art has been, and that may even be its most singular achievement—or its cardinal failure, depending on your point of view.

James Elkins, Professor of Art History, Theory and Criticism at the School of Art Institute of Chicago[37]

I need Art like I need God.

Tracey Emin, contemporary British artist[38]

I got introduced at a party last year as an artist and there was immediately an awkward silence. I think those around me were scared I might start talking about how lovely the reflection of light was off the profiteroles or something. Seeing the atmosphere around the table had turned cold, the host made a second attempt at introducing me which, at first, intrigued the gathered diners. Two jobs, eh? Superheroes have two jobs. She went on to explain that I was also employed by a Christian charity and was paid to evangelize people with the message of Jesus (I had just started a new job with the Universities and Colleges Christian Fellowship).

After an even longer excruciating silence one kind guest eventually offered, 'Is that landscapes or portraits you do?'

Not everybody, it seems, is happy to have an evangelical at their dinner party, which is odd when you think about how the word 'evangelical' basically

37. From his book On The Strange Place of Religion in Contemporary Art (New York: Routledge, 2004), p. 15.

38. Title of Tracey Emin's solo exhibition at the South London Gallery, 1998.

translates from the Greek as 'good news'. In a lecture given to the Royal College of Art in London on the subject of art and religion, artist and neurologist Jonathan Miller stated, 'Religion easily has the best bullshit story of all time',[39] going on to say, 'Personally, I don't see any reason why evangelical Christians feel they belong in academic institutions of art.' Miller's words, I believe, reflect an increasingly vocal and public opposition to those of sincere religious belief by many in positions of influence in the public sector.

I can sympathize with the broadcaster, presenter and self-proclaimed agnostic John Humphrys, who wrote in his book *In God We Doubt,* 'The atheists are on the march armed with much logic and even more righteous indignation at the horror of religion and determined, at the very least, to weaken its grip on the national debate.'[40]

So why so much scepticism?

I guess there's no easy answer to that question. It might have something to do with the postmodern, post-structuralist, post-whatever society we find ourselves in that rejects meta-narratives, institutional authority, absolute truth and notions of communication, language, text or something like that—apparently.

Perhaps for some, sincere belief in God is unreasonable, unintelligent or illogical, the concept of worshipping an ancient deity being outdated, twee or unenlightened. As Richard Dawkins puts it, 'faith is the great cop-out, the great excuse to evade the need to think and evaluate evidence.'[41]

Perhaps for others it's because of a negative personal experience of the church or even a poor demonstration of art from the church. I guess it's hard to take church seriously as an artist if you don't think the church really takes art seriously.

And why so few evangelicals in the arts?

The art historian and jazz critic Hans Rookmaaker once wrote, 'The artist who is a Christian struggles with great tensions ... an artist is expected to work from his own convictions but these may be seen by his atheist contemporaries as

39. *From personal notes taken at the lecture, 2008.*

40. In God We Doubt *(London: Hodder & Stoughton, 2007),* p. 16.

41. A Devil's Chaplain, *chapter 7:1 (London: Phoenix, 2003).*

ultra-conservative if not totally passé. On top of this he often lacks the support of his own community, his church and family.'[42] Rookmaaker wrote these words in 1946 but his evaluation still seems to fit, at least to some degree.

I am, by belief, an evangelical Christian yet I lament how rare it is to hear in evangelical churches a sermon preached on the subject of the arts, even though we are surrounded by music, writing, design and visual art on a daily basis.

I have often heard preachers at church be complimented on the clarity of their preaching. The trouble with artists is that we're often not very 'clear' in what we're trying to say, if we're trying to say anything at all—or if we even know what it is we want to say. The arts, by nature, play on concepts of mystery, ambiguity: appealing to the emotions and the imagination as well as to reason. A painting, song, play, novel or sculpture does not function in the same way as a sermon.

Evangelical and artist

So why aren't there more evangelicals in the creative arts? Why aren't there more artists in church? These questions are nuanced with years of debate and discourse between the church and the arts. Some may point to the European Reformation movement as the beginning of a shift away from the use of images in corporate worship within the Protestant tradition, although this line of argument is complex and it is important to remember that not all the early Reformers were opposed to art-making. Luther, particularly, was a great champion of the arts and, as we saw at the start of this book, even commissioned his friend Cranach the Elder to make an altar painting for his church in Wittenberg. Others may point towards the influence of the Enlightenment on the church and a move in the aesthetics of church practices from emotional or imaginative criteria to reason—but, again, the debate is complex.

One thing is for sure: it doesn't have to stay this way. I for one am not convinced that being a Christian is a handicap to working in the arts. We make opportunities through the strength of our work and graft. If we are misunderstood and misrepresented, didn't Jesus say we should expect that anyway? Better to remain faithful to God's calling that we should be Christ-like in all that we do—be that in our prayers, lifestyles, actions, speech or creativity.

42. *Introduction, Art Needs No Justification (Leicester: IVP, 2002), p. 9.*

Resources

There is no shortage of help out there for Christians working in the creative arts and media; it's just a case of knowing where to look. The following list is only a starting point: an edited list of resources we have found to be most helpful for students in UCCF and Interface Arts and arts graduates in Morphē. (Resources are listed alphabetically by title.)

Books

Art and Soul
By Hilary Brand and Adrienne Chaplin
Published by Piquant, Carlisle, 2001

Art and Soul is a foundational and highly practical introduction for Christians studying or working professionally in the creative arts. The authors begin with a potted history of Western art and culture from a Christian perspective, culminating in a brief evaluation of the postmodern condition. They draw application from a biblical framework of art practice that considers the cultural blueprint of the creation story, distortion of the fall and the hope for cultural renewal through the Spirit's work today and the new creation. Peppered with real-life case studies and plenty of images, *Art and Soul* is a great place to start if you're new to considering the issues facing Christians in the arts today.

Art and the Bible
By Francis Schaeffer
Published by IVP, Nottingham, 2009

This is a good starting point for any study of the biblical understanding of art and its function in God's Kingdom. Schaeffer introduces the Bible as a magnificent work of art in its own right as well as the Spirit-breathed revelation of God. He identifies helpful examples of artists in the Bible and art that pleased God as well as idolatrous art. Easy to read and full of well-crafted arguments, *Art and the Bible* is a modern classic. Also by the same author, *He is There* and *He Is Not Silent*.

Art in Action: Toward a Christian Aesthetic
By Nicholas Wolterstorff
Published by Wm. B. Eerdmans Publishing Company, Grand Rapids, MI, 2005

Nicholas Wolterstorff is Professor of Philosophy at Calvin College. Writing against what he sees as the predominantly Western notion that art exists merely for the purposes of aesthetic contemplation, Wolterstorff argues that a Christian perspective of art demands a more integrated approach for art-making to serve function in everyday life. His definition of art as an action, as opposed to a mere commodity to be bought and sold, is an important argument to be considered. This is a vigorous re-evaluation of art's function in society. A meaty read which some might find heavy going, but rewarding for those who stick with it to the end.

Art Needs No Justification

By Hans Rookmaaker

Published by UCCF: The Christian Unions, Leicester, 2002; also republished in *The Complete Works of Hans Rookmaaker,* published by Piquant in 2002–3

If you don't have time to work through *Modern Art and the Death of a Culture* you might want to have a go at this smaller work by the same author. Written as an encouragement to Christian artists and those who mentor Christians in the arts, this slim overview is a foundational introduction to the value of mere art-making as a wholly Christian activity. Highly readable. Highly applicable.

Bearing Fresh Olive Leaves

By Calvin Seerveld

Published by Piquant, Carlisle, 2000

A well-researched encouragement to all practising artists with Christian faith. The second chapter serves as something of a manifesto for why Christians should be working in the arts. Seerveld gives backbone to the argument that Christians are to pioneer, steward, collaborate, instruct and lead the way in the creative arts. Edited by art historian Nigel Halliday, *Bearing Fresh Olive Leaves* gives ideological wind to the sails of a healthy Christian practice of art. Still relevant. Still useful. A good book to read with a friend and discuss.

Creation Regained

By Albert M. Wolters

Published by Wm. B. Eerdmans Publishing Company, Cambridge, 2005

Albert Wolters's classic formulation of an integrated Christian worldview is foundational reading for any student keen to establish a biblical theology of work and creativity. He begins with 'What is a worldview?', outlining the influence of belief and the centrality of Scripture in establishing the way Christians view the world. Pinning his argument into the three basic categories in human history—creation, fall and redemption—Wolters helpfully identifies the importance of Christian participation in the world and our role in shaping and developing culture. Well researched and generously written, and a good introduction to the reformational biblical worldview.

He Is There and He Is Not Silent
By Francis Schaeffer
Published by Tyndale House Publishing House, 2001

The central volume in Francis Schaeffer's philosophical trilogy and first published in 1971, this book was a key text in empowering Christians' involvement in the arts. The trilogy maps the philosophical shifts from the Enlightenment period to the disturbing conclusions and final breakdown of the Great Modern project. Written well before Jean-François Lyotard published *The Postmodern Condition*, Schaeffer's classic masterpiece of Christian philosophical thought is remarkably prophetic concerning the times that would unfold after its publication and remains a staple nutrient in the diet of any Christian arts reader.

Imagine: A Vision for Christians in the Arts
By Steve Turner
Published by IVP, Nottingham, 2001

Fast becoming a contemporary classic, Steve Turner's *Imagine* reads like chicken soup to the soul of any Christian trying to make a go of it in the creative arts. As an experienced writer and poet, Turner has the credibility of a seasoned practitioner and the wisdom of a caring mentor. Easy to read, biblically grounded, beautifully written and highly applicable, this book speaks directly to Christian art practitioners with the authority of someone who has been there himself and knows the issues first-hand.

Modern Art and the Death of a Culture
By Hans Rookmaaker
Published by Crossway Books, Illinois, 1994; also republished in *The Complete Works of Hans Rookmaaker,* published by Piquant. Carlisle: 2002–3

Hans Rookmaaker is seen by many as the Great Grand-Daddy of Christian involvement in the arts. First published in 1970, at a time when the wider evangelical church actively discouraged Christian engagement in the arts, Rookmaaker's argument for an integrated understanding of art and art history is still relevant for Christians working in the creative arts today. As an art historian, Rookmaaker's grasp of the conceptual decline of Christian ethics since the Enlightenment is highly credible. Whilst his tone is primarily cautionary, the warmth of his concern for a Christian renewal in the arts is deeply inspiring. Os Guinness's review on the back cover reads, 'This is a landmark book for Christians in the arts.' He's not wrong.

On the Strange Place of Religion in Contemporary Art
By James Elkins
Published by Routledge, New York, 2004

James Elkins is Professor of Art History, Theory and Criticism at the School of Art Institute of Chicago and Head of the History of Art at University College, Cork, Ireland. Writing from an academic position outside the Christian subculture, Elkins is a credible voice in the wider discourse of art and faith. This pint-sized book asks why there are so few artists with authentic belief in God making work about their faith within the contemporary arts. He states, 'Contemporary Art, I think, is as far from organized religion as Western art has been, and that may even be its most singular achievement—or its cardinal failure, depending on your point of view', and suggests that it is impossible for those who express sincere belief in God to be taken seriously by the contemporary arts world. He argues that the arts are more tolerant of those who approach issues of faith with irony, scepticism or cynicism. Taking six students as examples of how notions of religious belief are articulated through contemporary art, Elkins illustrates the issues well and lays the foundation for a necessary discussion. Like Terry Eagleton, Boris Groys and Suzi Gablik, James Elkins's voice is an important contribution to the contemporary art/faith debate.

A Profound Weakness: Christians and Kitsch
By Betty Spackman
Published by Piquant, Carlisle, 2005

Witty, sincere, convincing and unique, Spackman's dissection of the Christian subculture obsession with kitsch is rigorously researched and utterly winsome. Funny and disturbing at the same time. *A Profound Weakness* is a book written by an artist for artists with a genuine concern for Christians to avoid the clichés and kitsch we are so often associated with. This book is one-of-a-kind, as thoughtfully presented as it is written. Since the book is crammed full of colour photos it retails at a high price but is worth every penny if your student budget can stretch to it. Extracts are available to buy from the Piquant Editions website for a more modest price.

Other books you might find helpful

The Artist's Yearbook / Writers' and Artists' Yearbook
Published annually in the summer by Thames and Hudson, and A&C Black, respectively.

Breath for the Bones—Art, Imagination and Spirit: a Reflection on Creativity and Faith
By Luci Shaw (Thomas Nelson, 2009)

Culture-Making: Recovering our Creative Calling
By Andy Crouch (IVP Books, 2008)

Reel Spirituality: Theology and Film in Dialogue
By Robert K Johnston (Baker Books, 2000)

Re-Sounding Truth: Christian Wisdom in the World of Music
By Jeremy S. Begbie (Baker Academic, 2007)

Walking on Water: Reflections on Faith and Art
By Madeleine L'Engle (H. Shaw, 1980 / NY: North Point Press, 1995)

Journals and Magazines

Image: A Journal of the Arts and Religion, ed. Gregory Wolfe
www.imagejournal.org

Third Way Magazine, ed. Simon Jones
www.thirdwaymagazine.co.uk

Websites

You can follow discussions related to this book at **www.beyondairguitar. blogspot.com**

There is also a website devoted to this book at
www.beyondairguitar.com

The home of the graduate arts network—with blogs, resources, events, project information and contacts—is at
www.morphearts.org

Other websites:

www.artisaninitiatives.org
International prayer network for Christians working in the creative arts and media with listings of regular events and gatherings.

www.artnet.com
Home of artnet international listings for exhibitions, galleries, artists and events.

www.artrabbit.com
Listings of exhibitions, job opportunities, awards, available artists grants and loans in the UK.

www.artscentregroup.org.uk
National network of Christians working professionally in the creative arts and media.

www.artway.eu
An informative website with links to European artists, events, arts organizations, museums and galleries. You can subscribe to regular email 'visual meditations'. The project is directed by Marleen Hengelaar-Rookmaaker and Laurel Gasque.

www.axisweb.org
Helpful listings of fine-arts projects, artists, exhibitions and opportunities in the wider field of the arts.

www.civa.org
Christians in the Visual Arts is a
USA-based arts organization with
a vision to equip those called to a
vocation in the visual arts; to help
the church embrace the visual arts
in worship and education; and to
influence contemporary culture
through serious art learning, practice
and prophetic engagement.

www.equity.org.uk
Equity is the website of the UK Trade
Union representing professional
performers and other creative
workers from across the spectrum
of the entertainment, creative and
cultural industries.

www.imago-arts.ca
A Canadian-based charity for
promoting and advocating the arts
in Canada. Imago is headed by
John Franklin and they produce a
triannual newsletter.

www.internationalartsmovement.org
Home of IAM, an arts organization
founded by the painter Makoto
Fujimura and based in New York to
encourage worldwide engagement in
creative cultural re-invigoration.

www.spotlight.com
Spotlight is a leading casting
resource that links casting directors
with performers and their agents.
Spotlight is used by most TV, Film,
Radio and Theatrical companies
throughout the UK, and many
worldwide.

www.uccf.org.uk
Use the links to find the Interface
Arts page with information about
student arts gatherings and
resources.

www.uk.castingcallpro.com
CastingCallPro is an online UK
directory of professional actors,
presenters, agents and casting
professionals.

ALSO VISIT

www.piquanteditions.com

Lightning Source UK Ltd.
Milton Keynes UK
UKOW07f0857200315

248215UK00005B/59/P